DATE DUE

Oct 4, 1995			
MAY 09 1996			
DEC 18 1996			
SE 24 '98			
SE 29 '98			
OCT 29 1998			
NOV 13 1998			
JA 27 '00			
GAYLORD			PRINTED IN U.S.A.

CULTURES OF THE WORLD

BRAZIL

Christopher Richard

MARSHALL CAVENDISH
New York • London • Sydney

Reference edition published 1992 by
Marshall Cavendish Corporation
2415 Jerusalem Avenue
North Bellmore
New York 11710

Editorial Director	Shirley Hew
Managing Editor	Shova Loh
Editors	Roseline Lum
	Siow Peng Han
	Leonard Lau
	MaryLee Knowlton
Picture Editor	Jane Duff
Production	Edmund Lam
Design	Tuck Loong
	Lee Woon Hong
	Dani Phoa
	Ong Su Ping
	Katherine Tan
Illustrator	Thomas Koh

Printed in Singapore

Library of Congress Cataloging-in-Publication Data:
Richard, Christopher, 1959–
  Brazil / Christopher Richard.
    p. cm.—(Cultures Of The World)
  Includes bibliographical references and index.
  Summary: Introduces the geography, history,
    culture, and lifestyles of Brazil.
  ISBN 1 85435 520 1
  1. Brazil. [1. Brazil.] I. Title. II. Series.
F2508.5.R53 1991
981—dc20   90-22471
                                  CIP
                                  AC

INTRODUCTION

Brazilians sometimes recount the tale of a contest between a farmer and an Indian to see who could spot the first ray of the rising sun. The farmer laughed when the Indian faced west, while he kept his eyes eastward. But he wheeled around in astonishment when the Indian declared: "There it is … the first ray!" Even before the sun had come up, its light had already reflected off a cloud in the western sky.

As the tale suggests, looking straight into the matter is not always the best way. Sometimes, it's better to focus first along the edges. This book tries to capture a few reflections of Brazil the same way. By providing a sampling, it will hopefully offer some insight into the diversity and vibrancy of this nation. If this book, part of the *Cultures of the World* series, triggers the reader to explore further, it will have done its job.

CONTENTS

A *candomblé* (religion with African roots) procession in the northern city of Salvador.

CONTENTS

**A Yanomami Indian in
the Amazon forest re-
serve.**

**Two young Brazilian
women having a win-
dowside chat.**

GEOGRAPHY

THERE ARE TWO WAYS to think about the immensity of Brazil and the wealth of its natural resources.

One is to use statistics. Brazil is the fifth largest and the sixth most-populated nation in the world. It has the world's longest continuous coastline. One quarter of all known plant species are found in Brazil, along with a third of the world's iron ore reserves. Scientists figure that the Amazon River and jungle produce one-third of the earth's oxygen and hold one-fifth of its fresh water reserves.

A second way is through the imagination. At the northeastern-most point of Brazil, you are closer to Africa than you are to its southern border. If you were to travel in a ship several miles up the Amazon River, you would have a hard time distinguishing the river from the ocean. The Amazon is 200 miles wide at its mouth and, at points 1,000 miles inland, seven miles wide.

No matter how you think about it, Brazil is not a country to ignore. This huge country can be divided into five regions.

The north and the central-west are regions with few people but great economic potential. The northeast holds much of Brazil's past history and most of its current poverty. The southeast and the south are home to most of its people and its wealth.

Opposite: **Spectacular Iguassu Falls was recently declared a Monument of Humanity by Unesco. It is two miles wide and pounds down 350-foot cliffs, sending sprays that accompany ever-present rainbows.**

Below: **Passengers from a yacht enjoy a secluded beach in the Angra Gulf, which has nearly 400 islands, 2,000 beaches, bays and coves and is a perfect marine life sanctuary.**

Waters of the Rio Negro, one of the Amazon's tributaries, mirror the jungle at dusk.

THE AMAZON

The north covers 40% of Brazil. On its own, this region would be the world's seventh largest nation. Two features dominate this region: the Amazon River and the Amazon jungle.

The Amazon River is the final link in a system of 1,000 rivers. Seventeen of these flow over 1,000 miles before they empty into it. It is the second-longest river in the world, but no other compares to it. Every second, it sends 80 million gallons of water into the Atlantic Ocean—that's more than the output of the next three biggest rivers in the world put together. Water from the Andes Mountains in the west, the Guiana Highlands in the north and Brazil's Central Plateau in the south empties into the Amazon. All told, the river drains an area almost the size of Australia.

The Amazon jungle covers most of this basin. Over the years, its mystery has attracted countless explorers. The Spaniards searched it for the mythical El Dorado, a city filled with gold, 400 years ago. They also created another myth, the story of a fierce tribe of women warriors called Amazons, which gave the area its name.

THE MIRACLE PLANTS

The first explorers who crossed the Andes Mountains found Indians using a white crystal taken from the bark of the *cinchona* tree as medicine. Hundreds of years later, scientists discovered that this crystal, called quinine, effectively protects people from the tropical disease of malaria.

Today, scientists called ethnobotanists believe that plants in the Amazon might hold a cure for acquired immune deficiency syndrome (AIDS), leukemia or cancer. They believe that the disappearing rain forests and the Indians who live in them should be protected, for they hold secrets which "civilized" people have yet to learn.

Ethnobotanists depend on the Indians' knowledge of the jungle just as much as they do on chemistry or biology. There are already examples of native medicine in use—street vendors in Manaus, the capital of the state of Amazonas, peddle various plants as cures for problems ranging from head lice to swollen intestines.

But scientists are now going beyond these city markets. They are exploring the jungle with Indian medicine men and observing the way they put plants to use; how a liquid squeezed from a fungus growing on dead trees can be used to treat ear aches, or tea made from a red berry can be used to fight fevers.

Do these potions cure, or are they just the superstitious imagination of primitive Indians? Perhaps these practices hold the key to finding another drug like quinine, and that is what the ethnobotanists hope to find.

Below: **Giant anteaters foraging for a tasty anthill.**

Bottom: **The capybara, the world's largest rat, takes a cool dip in a nearby river.**

Studying this jungle, people realize how much they have yet to discover. Explorers still find Indians who have never met an outsider. Scientists still find new kinds of insects and animals. Botanists believe the 25,000 plants cataloged represent only half of the jungle's total. Trees 200 feet high form an unbroken ceiling, blocking almost all light. Rivers criss-cross, and tropical storms frequently cause flooding.

Countless strange creatures exist among the Amazon's 10,000 known species: howler monkeys whose screams can be heard miles away; armies of ants that devour plants and animals as they advance; five-foot anteaters that can wipe out anthills with their snouts; or the five-foot, 150-pound capybara, the world's largest rat.

THE CENTRAL-WEST

The central-west contains four states and the Federal District of Brasília. The government built Brasília from scratch and made it the nation's capital in 1960, hoping that this would spur the region's development. The plan did not work out well. Brasília did grow, but the rest of the region did not. With almost two million residents, the Federal District has a population larger than three of the region's four states.

But in the 1970s, the central-west boomed. About 100,000 people moved in each year, giving it the reputation as Brazil's wild west. Landowners still hire *pistoleros* to keep squatters off their properties and guns often replace the law in frontier towns.

Almost all of the region sits on the Central Plateau, a huge plain 3,300 feet above sea level. Scrub brush and small trees cover most of the land, but rich, red soil lies underneath. The region has already become a major cattle raising area, and increasing amounts of land are being cultivated.

Many people fear that settlers pouring into the region will cause serious damage to the environment, which may alter the ecology of the entire world. Farmers use the "slash and burn" technique to prepare new fields. They cut down the vegetation, then burn it off. Satellites above the earth detect heat from thousands of small fires in the region, and scientists fear they contribute to the gradual warming of the planet.

Economic development also threatens the Pantanal, a low swampland off the Central Plateau along the Paraguay River. Pollution from mining and the growth of cattle herds endanger the fragile balance of this wildlife preserve along the border with Bolivia and Paraguay.

Rains flood the Pantanal between October and April. Over 350 types of fish thrive on the plants in the swollen rivers and spawn during this period. A dry season follows in which the water level falls and traps many fish in landlocked lakes. They make easy prey for the 600 species of birds who nest there at this time.

Alligators also thrive on these fish, but they are prey to human hunters. Poachers illegally killed about 1.5 million alligators in 1989. Man himself is not entirely safe. In open rivers, flesh-eating piranhas normally feed on small fish. But trapped in lakes during the dry season, they face a food shortage and may attack larger animals, even humans.

Beauty and the beast. An alligator in the evergreen Pantanal, a natural wildlife swampland covering 40,000 square miles.

Savana in the northern
state of Roraima.

THE NORTHEAST

Nine states along the Atlantic coast make up the northeast region holding 18% of Brazil's territory. This region, which was the first area the Portuguese colonized, is still a cultural center. It is also the poorest part of the country.

The climate is the main problem. Severe drought regularly plagues this region. The worst droughts came between 1877 and 1919, causing two million deaths. The most recent disaster, a five-year drought which ended in 1984, forced thousands to move to crowded cities or to the central-western frontier.

A narrow, fertile strip follows the coastline from the city of Natal south through Bahia. Here, cocoa and sugarcane plantations thrive if there is sufficient rain. A line of white sand beaches blesses this strip, making it

A farmer in the very dry northeast of Brazil. The interior of this region, called the *sertão*, is devastated with severe drought and poverty.

a popular spot for tourists. The major coastal cities of Recife, Maceió and Salvador all feature lots of history and beautiful beaches.

Beyond this lies the immense dry backland known as the *sertão*. Only cactus and shrub brush break up the dusty brown earth in this zone. Rain never falls during the first six months of the year. What rain there is comes in sudden storms—a few hours will produce most of the rainfall for an entire year. Flash floods are also a problem. Life is very difficult for the stubborn inhabitants of this region, many trying to squeeze out a living by raising cattle.

One major river, the São Francisco, breaks up the dreary scenery of the *sertão*. It serves as a source of transportation, water and energy. Barges and ferries patrol the 1,800-mile river, including an American steamboat built in 1913 for use on the Mississippi River. The river's water enables some farming to take place along its banks. At the Paulo Afonso dam and power plant in Bahia, it also generates electricity for much of the region.

A port in Rio de Janeiro with cars ready to be exported. Manufactured goods make up about 70% of Brazil's exports.

THE ECONOMIC PUMP

The southeast is the economic pump that keeps the country running. Made up of the states of Minas Gerais, Espirito Santo, Rio de Janeiro and São Paulo, it has only 11% of the nation's land, but holds the three largest cities (São Paulo, Rio de Janeiro and Belo Horizonte) and 44% of the total population.

São Paulo is the business capital of Brazil. It accounts for a third of the nation's industrial output. The third largest city in the world, its 10 million residents include immigrants from around the world. One million have ties with Italy, another million are of Lebanese descent, and the Japanese community numbers 600,000. Two million people have poured into the city from Brazil's northeast.

Brazilians fondly call Rio de Janeiro (population: 5.6 million) the *Cidade Maravilhosa*, or the Marvelous City. Sugar Loaf Mountain, a bare granite rock, majestically guards the entrance to Rio's scenic Guanabara Bay. A string of beautiful beaches, starting with Copacabana and Ipanema, follows the coastline outside the bay. Rio is still Brazil's top tourist attraction despite having lost its role as the leading business center and the nation's capital.

Belo Horizonte (population: 2.1 million) is the capital of Minas Gerais. Located on a high plateau about 2,500 feet above sea level, Minas Gerais has been an important mining center for 300 years. Three-quarters of the world's gold found in the 18th century came from Minas Gerias. Today, it is a major source of iron ore and valuable gems.

Most of the state of São Paulo sits on this same plateau. Here, the red soil and the temperate climate are perfect for growing coffee and this has financed the growth of São Paulo. Today, Brazil is by far the world's top exporter of coffee.

Rio de Janeiro—the Marvelous City—with Sugar Loaf Mountain, one of the world's most recognizable landmarks, towering over it.

THE SOUTH

The smallest of the five regions, the south is a cattle and agricultural center. Its three states all fall below the Tropic of Capricorn. Southerners are the only Brazilians who enjoy all four seasons. Snow occasionally falls in the hills of this region.

A low mountain range dominates the region, starting in the center of the state of Rio Grande do Sul and ending at the Central Plateau. The weather makes this area the first choice for many European immigrants. Only Germany's Munich has a bigger beer festival than the Oktoberfest organized by German immigrants in Blumenau, Santa Catarina. Italians brought grapes to South America and have started several vineyards in northern Rio Grande do Sul.

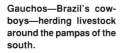

Gauchos—Brazil's cowboys—herding livestock around the pampas of the south.

A winter wonderland in Brazil. The south is the only region in Brazil that receives snowfall and frosts.

The south of Rio Grande do Sul is a flat grassland, an extension of the pampas of Argentina. This is still Brazil's main cattle raising area. Residents here are called gauchos, after the cowboys who round up the herds of the pampas.

The Paraná River dominates Brazil's third major river system. It joins the Paraguay River in Argentina before emptying into the Atlantic Ocean. This system features two wondrous sights, one natural and the other man-made. At the point where Brazil meets Argentina and Paraguay sits the Iguassu Falls. Water pouring over 275 waterfalls spread over a three-mile area produces a roar which can be heard several miles away. The most spectacular group is at the Devil's Throat, where 14 falls curve around a 350-foot drop.

Itiapú Dam, the heart of the world's largest hydroelectric plant, lies just a few miles from Iguassu Falls. It is a complex of five dams stretched over three miles. At its highest point, one dam soars more than a mile above the ground. The dam's reservoir is also Brazil's largest lake. Brazil and Paraguay joined in 1975 to build this project, located along the border between the two countries. It began generating electricity in 1984, but the whole complex will only be completed in late 1990.

HISTORY

THE PORTUGUESE SAILOR Pedro Alvares Cabral discovered Brazil in 1500, eight years after Columbus' discovery of America. Cabral had set off from Portugal for India via the coast of Africa. Many believed that he found South America by accident after winds blew him off his original course.

Modern historians have more faith in Cabral's navigational skills. They believe that the Portuguese suspected land lay to the west of Africa and sent Cabral to find it.

At this time, Spain and Portugal, being Europe's main imperial powers,

Above: **Portuguese colonists raising a cross while some of their comrades try to communicate with the native Indians.**

Opposite: **The historical town, Ouro Preto ("Black Gold") was the center of an 18th century gold rush. Today, it holds the country's purest baroque art collection and architecture. In 1981, Unesco declared it a World Cultural Monument.**

had sent explorers to the Americas, Africa and India. In 1494, the two countries signed the Treaty of Tordesillas, an agreement which would divide newly discovered lands between them. They drew a line through the Atlantic and agreed that lands found to the east of this line would belong to Portugal, while land to the west would fall to Spain.

If historians are right, the Portuguese were crafty in placing that line. When Cabral landed, he stood to the east of the land, giving Portugal a legal claim to part of Spanish America. He then sailed to India only two weeks later. Portugal did little to develop its new property, except for an occasional fleet visiting to collect some *pau brazil*. This wood, from which Europeans extracted red dye, gave the new colony its name.

THE INDIANS

According to findings in the state of Piaui, Brazil was already inhabited by a tribe of hunters as long as 47,000 years ago. Most experts, however, believe that these hunters made their way to Brazil via Asia and North America 12,000 years ago. These experts estimate that about four million natives were around when Pedro Cabral landed.

Colonizers from Europe did not bring prosperity and progress to the Indians, but new diseases such as measles and smallpox. Through these, the Portuguese unwittingly infected and killed thousands of Indians. They also tried to force the Indians to work on their sugar plantations. Unable to resist the Portuguese, many fled to the interior. Those who remained on the coast blended in through intermarriage with the Portuguese colonists and African slaves. Today, only about 220,000 Indians survive, almost all of them living in the Amazon region.

EXPANSION IN THE COLONIAL PERIOD

The Portuguese king paid little attention to Brazil until he realized other Europeans would take over the colony if he did not act. He handed out land titles, and in 1534 settlers founded the cities of Olinda and Vitoria. He then established a colonial government in the new city of Salvador da Bahia in 1549. In 1567, the Portuguese started the city of Rio de Janeiro on a site from which they had just expelled a group of French settlers.

In 1580, politics again boosted Brazil's development. Portugal became part of Spain, making Brazil a target for two of Spain's foes—Holland and France. The Dutch invaded and conquered parts of the northeastern coast between 1630 and 1654 while the French briefly seized what is now the state of Maranhão. The challenge of expelling these invaders brought more people to the colony. In 1625, 70 ships carrying more than 12,000 men sailed from Portugal to help the inhabitants fight the Dutch.

The growing number of settlers spurred exploration of Brazil's interior. The most colorful frontiersmen, called *bandeirantes* ("flag bearers"), led marches as far south as Argentina, as far west as Bolivia and as far north as the Amazon River. The *bandeirantes* established Brazil's claim to lands far west of the Treaty of Tordesillas agreement.

Orange Fortress on Itamaraca Island is a reminder of Brazil's colonial history.

THE BANDEIRANTES

When the *bandeirantes* set off from São Vincente (modern day São Paulo) at the end of the 16th century, their main purpose was not a noble one: they wanted to capture Indians to be sold as slaves. The Indians of the northeast fled inland to escape. Ironically, the *bandeirantes* depended on Indians to guide them on their trips. Some tribes helped the hunters capture rival tribes.

Antonio Raposo Tavares was one of the most famous *bandeirantes*. In 1648, he set out from São Vincente with 200 colonists and 1,000 Indians. He destroyed several Jesuit missions along the Paraguayan border, sending the Indians who lived in them off to slavery. He then proceeded north along the Paraguay River until he reached territories that now lie in Bolivia. From there, he followed the Madeira River and then the Amazon until he reached the Atlantic. In 1651, after traveling more than 3,000 miles, he returned with only 59 men.

As time passed and the increase in African slaves took the profit out of their original business, the *bandeirantes* began prospecting for gold. They found it in Minas Gerais in 1693, setting off a gold rush which drew thousands of settlers to Brazil's center.

The monument to the *bandeirantes* in São Paulo. They were considered the all-purpose frontiersmen, who usually had European fathers and Indian mothers. From his Indian heritage, the *bandeirante* had superb scouting and survival skills; from his European side, he had a hunger for gain and an adventurer's streak that would send him roaming the entire country.

SLAVERY IN BRAZIL

Slaves from Africa played just as big a part in Brazil's development as Portuguese colonists. As early as 1516, slaves began arriving, and before the slave trade was abolished, about 3.6 million came. At the time of independence in 1822, an estimated two million made up over half the population.

The slaves did not submit willingly to their fate. Many ran away from their "masters" to the unsettled hills of the interior where they formed independent colonies called *quilombos*. The most famous, Quilombo dos Palmares, had a population of 30,000. It survived for 76 years before it was crushed in 1694 by an army.

After Brazil gained independence, a movement to end slavery slowly grew. The emperor's daughter, Princess Isabel, took the final steps in implementing it. In 1871, while her father was away, she convinced the Brazilian Congress to grant freedom at birth to the children of slaves. Then in 1889, she passed a law which freed the last slaves. Brazil was the last country in the Western Hemisphere to abolish slavery.

INDEPENDENCE AND EMPIRE

Events in Europe set the stage for independence. In 1807, Napoleon's army conquered Portugal. King João fled to Rio de Janeiro, making Brazil the only colony ever to become the seat of power for an empire. Before returning to Portugal 14 years later, King João established an effective system of government and left his son, Dom Pedro, to rule Brazil.

When King João got back to the mother country, he found a hostile parliament insisting that Brazil be ruled from Lisbon. It demanded the return of Dom Pedro. Judging that the Brazilians would fight for independence rather than return to colonial status, Dom Pedro decided to stay. On September 7, 1822, he proclaimed Brazil's independence. Three months later, he was crowned the "constitutional emperor and perpetual defender" of Latin America's only empire.

The perpetual defender lasted only nine years. Brazilians wanted more popular participation in government but Dom Pedro ruled as an absolute monarch. He fought constantly with the new Brazilian Congress and lost popular support when Brazil lost southern territories in a war against Argentina. In 1831, Dom Pedro abdicated and returned to Portugal. He left behind as heir his 6-year-old son, Dom Pedro II.

REIGN OF DOM PEDRO II

Following Dom Pedro's departure, rebellions broke out in the northeast and in the south, and the country appeared on the brink of disintegration. In 1840, Congress turned in desperation to Dom Pedro II and made the 15-year-old ruler of Brazil.

Incredibly, Dom Pedro II proved equal to the task. His 49-year rule marked the most stable and progressive stretch in Brazil's history. He granted more power to the Congress, but used his authority and personal prestige to keep the upper hand in government.

The emperor encouraged agricultural growth and immigration. As a result, by 1888, over 100,000 Europeans were immigrating annually to the southeast of Brazil. Most of them went to work on coffee plantations in São Paulo, as coffee by that time made up well over half of the country's exports.

Dom Pedro II firmly established Brazil's southern borders through battles with neighbors. The hardest struggle started in 1865. It took five years for Brazil, allied with Uruguay and Argentina, to defeat Paraguay in this war.

These campaigns increased the size and stature of the army. Military officers began to involve themselves in politics, a development which eventually led to the emperor's downfall. In the 20th century, the military would become Brazil's most powerful political institution.

Emperor Dom Pedro II. This extraordinary but always humble man brought much-needed peace to Brazil, giving it the longest continuous period of political stability. He did not adopt the autocratic ways of his father, but guided the nation with personal authority. Sadly, Brazil's most popular leader was forced into exile in 1889 when the military overthrew his government.

Getúlio Vargas represented the total break from Brazil's previous rural-controlled politics. Instead, politics began to be dominated by the people from Brazil's fast-growing urban areas.

THE REPUBLIC

The prosperous era of Dom Pedro II ended in November 1889. Having lost the support of the landowners through the abolition of slavery, he could not resist a revolt led by the military. He went into exile and the military proclaimed a new republic of the United States of Brazil.

Forty disorderly years followed. The republic had a president and a Congress, as well as regular elections. But conflicting regional interests made their jobs difficult, and the military continued to play an active role in politics. Between 1889 and 1930, 13 presidents held office.

In 1930, a military coup placed a civilian from the state of Rio Grande do Sul, Getúlio Vargas, in power. He represented a new kind of leader: a populist who depended on the support of the urban masses instead of the rich landowners. Vargas legalized labor unions, passed a minimum wage law and instituted a social security system. He also made himself a dictator, first by rewriting the constitution, then by canceling elections. In 1945, the same institution that brought him to the top staged a coup to oust him and restore democracy.

RULE BY THE MILITARY

In the 1950s, vast sums of money were spent on building Brasília as well as hydroelectric plants, highways and other economic projects. It set the stage for future growth, but also brought immediate economic problems by placing the nation in debt. It led to yet another coup, but this time the military kept power. From 1964 to 1985, five army generals ruled.

At first the military enjoyed great support. The 1970s was the decade of the Brazilian Miracle, when industry grew at spectacular rates and provided thousands of jobs. But political freedom disappeared. Thousands of people were forced into exile or arrested on political grounds.

BRAZIL IN THE SECOND WORLD WAR

When Brazil declared war on Germany in 1942, it became the first South American country to enter the conflict. The 25,000-strong Brazilian Expeditionary Force that went to Italy in 1944 was the first South American army to engage in battle overseas. The force served until the end of the war under the command of the U.S. Fifth Army.

Another contribution was the airfield in Natal, in the northeast. Most aircraft at that time could not fly non-stop across the Atlantic; in 1942, U.S. planes made Natal an immediate stop on their way to providing supplies to Allied troops in North Africa, the Middle East and even China. Brazil had entered the war because it felt that with its size and resources, it needed to play a role in world affairs. The country made worthy and immensely vital contributions to the ending of the war.

The economy stopped growing in the 1980s and Brazil again found itself unable to pay back its loans. Frustrated by the debt and by growing public discontent, the military handed power back to a civilian president in 1985. In 1989, 100 years after the proclamation of the republic, the people elected Fernando Collor de Mello as their new president.

GOVERNMENT

WHEN FERNANDO COLLOR DE MELLO took office as president in March 1990, the structure of the Brazilian government closely resembled that of the United States. Its foundation, however, was nowhere near as solid.

Since its independence in 1822, its leaders have rewritten the constitution seven times. The latest version came into effect on October 5, 1988, but its future was already in doubt. A "self-destruct" clause in it calls for a vote to be held in 1993 to decide whether Brazil should switch from a federal to a European-style parliamentary system.

Since the 1950s, Brazil's president has dominated the Congress. During the years of military dictatorship, Congress lost all its power. Many Brazilians think a parliamentary system might help balance the powers of the executive and legislative branches.

For now, the 1988 constitution keeps the president strong. He needs congressional approval for many acts, but he in turn can veto laws passed by Congress. Collor inherited control of many government agencies: 23 ministries (compared to 13 in the United States) and 188 state-owned companies.

The president also plays an important role in state politics. He has the power to intervene in state affairs, calling in federal troops if he feels they are necessary. The states cannot levy taxes on their own, so they depend on the president to finance their budgets.

On paper, Brazil is a full democracy. All citizens between 17 and 70 who can read must vote. Voting is voluntary for teenagers, senior citizens over 70 and the illiterate.

Above: **Fernando Collor de Mello, elected president of Brazil in 1989.**

Opposite: **Swans swim along a pool reflecting the government buildings of Brasília. The capital was the brainchild of Juscelino Kubitschek, who served as president in the 1950s. While it showed the dynamism of Kubitschek's administration, it also drained the country of much of its money, leaving huge debts and high inflation.**

THE BASICS OF GOVERNMENT

Brazil is a federal republic made up of 26 states and one federal district. The government is divided into the executive, legislative and judicial branches. The president and his cabinet make up the executive branch. The president serves a five-year term and cannot be re-elected.

The legislature consists of a Congress divided into two bodies, a Senate and a Chamber of Deputies. The Senate has 72 members, three elected from each state (two newly-created states have yet to elect their representatives), while the Chamber has 487 deputies, at least three from each state. Senators serve eight-year terms while deputies hold office for four years. Both can run for re-election. Each state has an elected governor and legislature. States are divided into counties called *municipios*, each of which is directed by an elected mayor.

The judiciary is more complicated. An 11-member Supreme Court has the final say in all legal matters. Federal and state courts fall below the Supreme Court. Special federal courts handle cases in certain specialized areas like labor, military, juvenile and election issues.

The 1988 constitution protects several rights for citizens: the freedom of speech, the freedom of the press, the freedom to assemble peacefully, and the freedom for workers to strike. It also permits citizens to require the government to release all information it has gathered on them. The latest change of the constitution gave Indians full rights as citizens for the first time, and guaranteed Indian tribes the rights to all resources falling within their land.

ARMY COLONELS

Two types of "colonels" complicate the operation of Brazil's democracy. The first are officers of the military. In the last 100 years, they have become Brazil's strongest political institution. All officers are taught that it is their duty to ensure the nation's security, and have in the past intervened in instances they considered a threat to law and order.

Since the 1940s, the military has stood watch against any movement connected in the slightest way with communism. They took over the government in 1964 because they believed the president planned to make himself a communist dictator.

After 21 years in power, the military gave up the presidency to a civilian, publicly guaranteeing that they would not get involved in politics again. But Brazilians know that the threat of intervention still exists.

The power of the military is undeniable in Brazilian politics. The armed forces ruled Brazil from 1964 to the mid-1980s. However, in the late 1980s, they ran out of ideas and patience to help solve the country's runaway economic debt, finally turning to civilian politicians for help.

HONORARY COLONELS

The second type of "colonel" has nothing to do with the military. His origins date back to 1850, when state governments depended on the National Guard to maintain law and order in Brazil's northeast. The wealthy landowners competed for the prestige of being named the colonel in charge.

These colonels became the most important political leaders in their counties. They were the chief law enforcers and the supervisors of general elections. They also served as the government's main source of local news as well as its main supporter in the region. They became the middlemen between the government, which depended on them to deliver election votes, and the voters, who depended on them to get what they needed from the government.

As time passed, the National Guard lost its importance and the colonels disappeared. But honorary colonels remain. The wealthiest and most influential men are called colonels.

These men are still the main link between the capital and the countryside. They provide the votes for the governor, who repays with special favors. In a land of low education and pay, citizens vote for the colonel's people because they believe if they help the colonel, he may return the favor.

MODERN POLITICS

The country colonels have dominated Brazilian politics for 150 years. But there are signs that their importance is fading.

Most Brazilians now live in cities, so the rural vote has lost some of its importance. The colonels also associated themselves with the military

Brazilians tell of one town in the state of Pernambuco which has been run by the same family since 1848. At the start of the 1980s, the mayor was the cousin of the district judge, who was the cousin of the civil registrar, who was the cousin of the former public prosecutor, who was the cousin of the district's congressman.

government, and lost prestige along with the army generals when they gave up power. Finally, the growth of the media has made it harder for the colonels to manipulate voters.

Before the spread of radio and television, Brazilians living outside the cities only knew the local news. Since the colonel dominated the news, they usually saw fit to vote as the colonels wished. Now they are more aware of national issues, and of people who are more powerful.

Before, election candidates could only reach voters through the colonels. Now they can speak directly to all via radio and television. This has led to the growth of national political parties, the largest being the Brazilian Democratic Movement (PMDB), which won more than half the votes in the 1986 elections.

Brazilians, young and old, celebrate at a political rally in Rio de Janeiro.

PATRONAGE

In modern Brazil, politics still revolve around people, not parties. In the 1989 presidential elections, the PMDB candidate finished far behind Collor de Mello, who overcame the weakness of his party with his charismatic personality and was able to impress voters and form alliances with local leaders.

In the eyes of voters, having friends in the right places is generally more useful than having good ideas. Leaders with good ideas aren't good candidates if they can't get anything done. And to get things done, they have to know people and be able to make deals.

In his first test, Collor de Mello got things done; when the senate voted on his measures, 45 of 54 votes came in his favor from PMDB senators.

31

ECONOMY

"NOBODY HOLDS BACK THIS COUNTRY!" So proclaimed a popular Brazilian slogan in the 1970s. The economy boomed during that decade, and the people believed their country was destined to become a major world power. The sleeping giant, they said, has finally awoken.

There was, and still is, much evidence to support this belief. In the 1950s, most Brazilians lived and worked in the countryside. Now, three-fourths of the population live in the cities. Then, Brazil depended on coffee for more than half its exports. Now, industrial goods like cars and airplanes make up two-thirds of all exports, and soybeans have replaced coffee as the main agricultural export.

Brazil could well undergo equal change over the next 30 years. The population is now concentrated in the southeast, but migration to the north and central-west has started. Major deposits of gold, iron ore and various minerals await exploitation in these regions, to say nothing of the possibilities of farming and ranching.

In the 1970s, the years of the Brazilian Miracle, the government spent billions of dollars on projects like the Trans Amazon Highway, underground subways for Rio de Janeiro and São Paulo, and a nuclear power plant. Growth has slowed in the 1980s, but industrial technology continues to advance. The government is designing a rocket to launch a Brazilian-made satellite. Alcohol distilled from sugarcane has replaced gasoline as the fuel for most new Brazilian cars.

Above: **A link across the heart of the Amazon. The Trans Amazon Highway cuts through the jungle to as far as the eye can see.**

Opposite: **Huge cranes tower over the docks of a Rio de Janeiro port. Thanks to massive foreign investments by multinational companies, Brazil emerged as one of the world's largest economies.**

THE PROBLEM

Despite tremendous progress in the last 30 years, life for most Brazilians has not improved. The majority of people do not share the nation's wealth. Over half of the workers earn less than $170 each month. Together, they earn less than the richest 1% of society.

In the northeast, people have a life expectancy of 55, while those in the southeast live up to 67. Eight out of 10 northeastern children suffer from malnutrition.

Every major city has its share of slums, called *favelas*, on the fringes of a city. About two-fifths of the residents of Rio de Janeiro live in *favelas*. By the age of 13, most slum children are on the streets shining shoes, selling gum, begging or stealing. Children in *favelas* have little chance of acquiring an education or a well-paying job. Changing this pattern is the biggest challenge facing Brazil today.

A child peddling products in the city—one of Brazil's saddest sights. Thousands of homeless children have to fend for themselves because their parents could not afford to keep them at home.

THE FIGURES

Here is a sampling of the diversity and scale of Brazil's economy, the eighth largest in the world. It is also the:
—largest exporter of coffee and orange juice
—2nd largest producer of soybeans, cocoa, tin and iron ore
—3rd largest producer of corn and bauxide
—5th largest producer of gold and exporter of military weapons
—7th largest producer of steel
—9th largest car manufacturer
Brazil is also a world leader in one very undesirable category: it owes foreign banks $115 billion, the largest debt of any developing country. That means every man, woman and child owes more than $750,000.

GOLD RUSH!

The government sees the north and central-west as the answer to its problems. The recent discovery of gold has drawn thousands into these regions.

Brazil's most famous discovery came in 1979 at Serra Pelada. The miners, called *garimpeiros*, are independent. Struggling through piles of mud like ants streaming around an anthill, they carry about 25 tons of dirt out of the mine each year.

Serra Pelada is not the only place where gold has been found. Prospectors have also become rich in the Rondônia and Roraima rivers. Major deposits in Roraima, along the Venezuelan border, have caused problems; they are located near the Yanomami Indian Reservation. The government has prohibited *garimpeiros* from working there, but so far, the lure of gold has outweighed such laws.

Besides invading Indian land, the *garimpeiros* cause other problems. They use mercury to separate gold from the soil, thereby polluting rivers and poisoning themselves. They work in unhealthy conditions and are cut down by tropical diseases. They have only their guile to protect their claims, and must take care lest tricky businessmen con them out of their gold.

Still, the mining continues. In the hills of Pará and the river banks of the Roraima and Rondônia, hope lives. *Garimpeiros* believe that anyone can become rich with the right combination of hard work and luck.

The gold camp of Serra Pelada; officials estimate that about two-thirds of the gold is smuggled out of the country.

Harvesting sugarcane.

FARMLAND

The future is not as bright for farmers moving north. The government began granting settlers in Rondônia 247-acre plots of land. It quickly had a waiting list of 20,000 families and had to stop taking applications. Those who got land usually sold it within a few years. Wealthy landowners bought the land and established huge farms and ranches.

The land being opened up follows the pattern established in the rest of the country. A quarter of all Brazilians live in the countryside, but few of them till their own land. About 5% of the population owns 80% of the land. The government has tried to change this with a law that allows it to buy private property that is not being used and give it to those who have no land. The law has satisfied no one. Landowners feel the government's payment falls far below the value of the property, and peasants are unhappy because they feel the government is too slow in enforcing it. Some have tried occupying unused property, but landowners have responded by hiring gunmen to keep them off. The result has been disastrous; in 1988, battles between the two sides killed hundreds.

The assembly line of AMX jets in São Paulo. Brazil is one of the largest manufacturers of military weapons in the world.

THE INDUSTRY

While the government has tried to encourage people to move to the country's interior, its main objective for the last 30 years has been to promote Brazilian industry.

Billions of dollars have been borrowed for projects supporting industries. Foreign companies have been invited to build plants, and high tariffs were created to discourage people from buying foreign products. The government also established state-run companies which dominate key industries such as oil, steel, communications and electricity.

Originally, the goal was to reduce the country's dependence on foreigners by making more products at home. The loans soon made another goal more important: to export goods for money needed to pay the nation's debt. Brazilian industry responded to this goal, and Brazilian-made products can be found throughout the world: cars, computers, tanks, shoes.

In 1988, the country's trade surplus surpassed $19 billion. Today, trade and industry support the vast majority of workers. Over 40 million people hold regular jobs in the cities.

A large grain ship with its cargo of soybeans ready for export.

INFLATION

"The only thing that ever goes down here is the value of my money," is a common complaint in Brazil. For the last several years, prices have risen every day. The price of meat doubled in Rio de Janeiro in February 1990. That made it 27 times more expensive than it was in February 1989.

The meteoric fall in the value of Brazil's money in 1989 prompted the president to take immediate action. He took three zeroes off the value of the bills and gave them a different name. So 1,000 new *cruzados* suddenly became one *cruzeiro*.

The president was following an old routine which started in 1942, when the *cruzeiro* was created to take the place of the *real*. The *cruzeiro* lasted until 1965 when it was declared to have one-one thousandth the value of the new *cruzeiro*, which gave way to the *cruzado* in 1986, which in turn was replaced by the new *cruzado* in 1989. In the 1980s, many Brazilians were millionaires, but their *cruzeiros* and *cruzados* were not worth much.

Brazil's leaders have long feared that measures needed to stop this would bring worse hardships, but the new president risked this with drastic action in 1990. It remains to be seen if he will succeed in ending Brazil's long war with inflation.

Until he took office, the government had been adjusting minimum wages based on the monthly rate of inflation. But wages and savings never quite kept up with inflation, so people looked for other ways to avoid losing money.

One way was to use their money to buy currency that did not fall in value. For example, people were so desperate to trade their cash for American dollars that they sometimes paid more than twice the official exchange rate.

Workers placing wood to be exported in a containing area in Belem Harbor.

BRAZILIANS

OUTSIDE OF ISOLATED INDIANS in the Amazon and recent immigrants from Europe or Asia, few Brazilians can honestly claim to have ethnically pure blood.

For 400 years, Africans, Indians and Europeans have melded together in Brazil to create countless combinations of skin colors.

Simple words exist to describe the first generation coming from these mixed couples: African and European parents produce mulattos. *Caboclo* children have European and Indian blood, while the offspring of an African and an Indian is called a *cafuso*. But once mulattos, *cafusos* and *caboclos* mix with Europeans, the process of scientific definition becomes more complicated.

Scientists "estimate" that about half of all Brazilians are white, another quarter are mulatto, while blacks and mixed Indians each make up about a tenth of the population.

Despite being a racial melting pot, Brazil is still marked by strong regional differences. In general, the European influence is stronger in the south and southeast, while the African culture dominates the states of Bahia and Rio de Janeiro as well as much of the northeast. Indian traditions and Indian blood have left their marks in the northeast's *sertão*, and in the northern and central-western regions.

Above: **Over 60 years of experience show on the faces of these two elderly Brazilians.**

Opposite: **A little *caboclo* girl inches by the doorway in Rio Padaouari.**

POPULATION DISTRIBUTION

At its current growth rate of 2%, Brazil's population of 148 million will double in 34 years. Most of the people are young; two-thirds of all Brazilians are below 30. Many argue that a growing population is needed to colonize the interior regions. But while more people are moving there, the crowded cities on the coast are absorbing most of the growth. São Paulo mushroomed from 3.8 million people in 1960 to 10.1 million in 1985. One out of five Brazilians live in the metropolitan areas of São Paulo, Rio de Janeiro or Belo Horizonte, the three largest cities.

The distribution of population in Brazil.

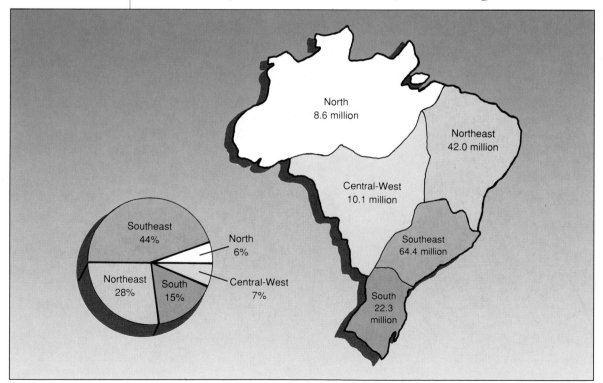

A mother with her two children in a shantytown in Salvador. Though they make up more than 40% of Brazil's population, blacks suffer from discrimination. They are still quietly barred from some restaurants and hotels, or told to enter a building by the back way. The country's leading civil rights advocates, clergymen and churches are fighting to bring such barriers down.

DISCRIMINATION

Brazil's constitution prohibits racial discrimination, and Brazilians are proud of the absence of racial strife in their country. But this peace does not mean that there is racial equality.

Few dark-skinned men or women are found in the Congress, or among army generals, corporate presidents and diplomats. The average income and education of blacks fall far below those of lighter-skinned Brazilians.

Since most blacks come from the impoverished northeast, many argue that this reflects the lack of opportunities for Brazil's poor rather than racial discrimination. Whether it is because of racism or not, most Brazilians associate dark skin with the lower classes, and this leads to discrimination against blacks.

Still, whites and blacks intermarry frequently. Experts disagree on the exact numbers, but agree that over the past 40 years the number of *mulattos* has greatly increased while the percentage of whites and blacks in the total population has dropped.

THE INDIANS

Today, almost all of Brazil's remaining 220,000 Indians live in the Amazon. The jungle still serves as a barrier isolating them from the modern world. Civilization, however, is breaking through. Brazilians face the challenge of integrating Indians into society without destroying the Indian culture.

In 1961, the government's National Foundation for Assistance to Indians created the Xingu National Park. Here, officials try gradually to introduce modern tools and ideas to the Indians. Some Indians are making the leap into the Brazil of today. In 1982, a leader of the Xingu tribe was elected into the National Congress.

Still, experts are not optimistic about the chances of preserving Indian traditions. Open land and the promise of gold have settlers pouring into Indian territories. Like the European colonists 500 years ago, they thrust new diseases and unfamiliar ideas upon the Indians. Unlike their ancestors, today's Indians have nowhere to flee; like their ancestors who stayed, they will most likely be absorbed into the mainstream of society or die.

SAO PAULO: COSMOPOLITAN CENTER

More than any other city, São Paulo reflects Brazil's history as a nation of immigrants. For the past century, it has attracted the bulk of the country's European and Asian immigrants. It currently draws most of the rural peasants flocking to the cities in search of better opportunities.

Thousands of these migrants, mostly from the northeast, live in the neighborhood of Bras. Walking through Bras, you can hear the music of *violeiros*, northeastern fiddlers who spontaneously compose songs on any subject in response to challenges from their audience; and you can see salesmen on streets peddling alligator skins and Amazon herbs.

The future of his people—this young Indian and others like him hope to raise the consciousness of the nation to the plight of their people.

Close by, in the neighborhood of Bom Retiro, Moslems, Jews and Christians peacefully live in the thriving middle-eastern shopping district. They are the descendants of immigrants from Lebanon, Syria and Turkey who did not bring the hostility of their homeland with them.

One million São Paulo residents of Italian descent live in the Bela Vista neighborhood. A string of European-style *cantinas* lie in the heart of this Little Italy. Every August, they hold a festival to remember their homeland, drinking 1,300 gallons of wine, three tons of spaghetti and 40,000 pizzas.

Liberdade is home to most of São Paulo's 600,000 *nissei* (sons) and *sansei* (grandsons) of Japanese immigrants. Signs advertise in Japanese and residents buy three local Japanese papers. Buddhist altars and judo classes are offered, and restaurants serve Oriental food to customers seated on the floor eating with chopsticks off low wooden tables.

Under two flags: this Japanese immigrant shows which countries she supports. In 1908, the immigrant ship *Kasato Maru* arrived in Santos Harbor with the first of 250,000 Japanese. They were seeking a new place to call home, away from the crop failures and earthquakes in their native land. Today, they dominate São Paulo's Liberdade district.

AMERICANA

A unique group of immigrants founded the city of Americana, about an hour's drive from São Paulo. The city's seal tells its history: it features the stars and bars insignia of the Confederate States of America, flanked by two soldiers wearing the uniforms of the Confederate Army.

After the end of the American Civil War in 1865, about three million Southerners from the defeated Confederate states left America. A handful ended up in Brazil, where they started several settlements. Americana is the most prominent of the surviving settlements.

While most of its current 160,000 residents are descendants of later European immigrants, its Confederate heritage is obvious. Walking down the streets, you can still occasionally hear English spoken with a Southern accent. A monument in the downtown area honors Confederate soldiers who died in the Civil War. Near by stands a cemetery with the graves of Confederate immigrants.

TYPICAL BRAZILIAN FIGURES

THE *VAQUEIRO* He is a cowboy who tends herds in the arid northeastern *sertão*. He is the descendant of African slaves and Portuguese settlers who left the coast and mixed with the Indians of the interior. He is stoic and struggles to survive in a hostile environment. Few amusements break up the monotony of his work, but annual round-ups and occasional rodeos offer him a chance to get together with others and show off his skills. Quiet, unemotional but patient, he carries on with life. He is not so much a fighter as a survivor.

THE GAUCHO He is the cowboy of the south. Life on the pampas is easier for him, and he is a more colorful figure. Like his cousins in Argentina, Uruguay and Paraguay, his forefathers came from Spain and took Indian wives. At first they were outlaws who roamed the countryside, but they gained fame by helping in Argentina's fight for independence from Spain. Today, he is the symbol of macho self-sufficiency. Loud and abusive, he is used to getting his way. He will brag about his three most prized possessions: his horse, his knife and his wife. Known for his riding skills, he is also noted for the bitter *mate* tea which he brews, and the grilled *churrasco* meat which he barbecues.

A *baiana* (woman from Bahia) in her native dress.

THE SUYA This tribe is typical of the native Indians in Brazil. The lip discs, a disc placed in the lower lip, is a trademark of some Amazon-based tribes. The Suya primarily fish and cultivate cassava plants. Because the Amazon soil is too thin to support extensive farming, they generally live in small groups of about 60, with three or four families sharing all they grow or catch. Every two or three years, after exhausting the soil in one area, they move to a new patch of the forest.

THE *BAIANA* Perhaps the most powerful symbol of Brazil's African heritage, *baiana* means a resident of Bahia, the state which had the largest population of slaves. In popular usage it refers specifically to black women dressed in the traditional white clothing of their ancestors. They can be seen every day on the city streets selling tasty food. They play a role on special occasions like Salvador's festival of Our Lord of Bonfim or during the Carnival in Rio de Janeiro.

LIFESTYLE

A SÃO PAULO TELEVISION CREW went to interview a homeless family that lived under a highway overpass. These immigrants from the northeast survived by rummaging through garbage cans for empty bottles or old newspapers to sell.

Asked how he was getting along, the father said he was happy, and added "thanks be to God." The astonished interviewer asked what he had to be happy about. The father replied that his family could play cards together at night, or sing and dance together, and they had a transistor radio so they could listen to soccer games.

Brazilians constantly amaze outsiders with their ability to look on the bright side of life. A resigned outlook on life makes their optimism even more remarkable. The Protestant work ethic does not thrive in Brazil. Hard work and good intentions, in the view of most citizens, are not enough to change things. Brazilians firmly believe that authorities greater than any individual control society, and that powers greater than people control destiny. Any human effort without the support of these higher forces will inevitably fail. It's no wonder Brazilians end most declarations by adding, "if God wishes."

But Brazilians also believe that higher authorities are flexible. This is the secret to their good cheer. The proper amount of cleverness, respect and patience will eventually soften the commands of anyone, from the local police captain to the president of the republic. And no matter how un-Christian their behavior, Brazilians believe they can gain God's forgiveness through proper repentance and prayer. After all, popular wisdom holds that God is a Brazilian.

Above: **The communal house of the Yanomami Indians sits like a UFO in the middle of the Amazon forest.**

Opposite: **São Paulo's biggest shopping center, the Eldorado, is a huge glass-enclosed building of mirrors and fountains.**

"WE'LL FIND A WAY"

Flexible rules make getting things done a tricky, inexact science. *Jeito* is the word used to describe this science. The word means "way," but to a Brazilian, it means much, much more.

Someone described as *jeitoso* is a master of squirming out of difficult situations and solving complicated problems. When most people say some goal is impossible, this clever person will promise to *dar um jeito* or to find a way. The key to *jeito* is knowing when and how to bend rules. Sometimes following rules makes good sense, or the authority behind the rule is strong enough to force compliance. Other times, rules are just pointless obstacles that can and should be avoided.

Traffic laws offer a good example of this attitude. For Brazilian drivers in cities like Rio de Janeiro, a red traffic light does not mean STOP. It means stop if there is likely to be traffic. Late at night, when the streets are deserted, they see no reason to stop and rarely do so.

In the larger cities, motorists often pull right onto the sidewalk to park. The law prohibits this, of course, and periodically the government embarks on campaigns to keep the sidewalks for pedestrians. Drivers, though, know that sidewalk parking makes sense because the number of cars far surpasses the number of legal parking spots. They also know that the police have better things to do than issue traffic tickets.

Two men having a chat outside a bar.

MIDDLEMEN

Compromise is a part of daily life in Brazil. Merchants and customers bargain over prices, taxi drivers and riders haggle over fares. In an extreme example, thieves sometimes negotiate with their victims to determine a price for their stolen belongings! While Brazilians take pride in their ability to negotiate, many situations require outside help. Here, the middleman plays an important role.

Brazilian Catholics pray to their patron saints in a hope to win them as allies. When they have problems, they can then count on him (or her) to intercede with God on their behalf. The political equivalent to the saint is the "colonel." The most influential citizen in rural communities, people support the candidate he supports during elections because they know he can request help from the elected person on their behalf.

Businessmen rely on a "fixer," called a *despachante*, to deal with Brazil's relaxed attitude toward deadlines. The *despachante* takes care of routine, everyday jobs. He might ask a relative who works for the trade ministry to speed up his employer's application for a license, or an influential friend to make phone calls on behalf of his client. Brazilians lament the corruption, but it is a way of getting many things done.

FAMILY TIES

As this reliance on personal ties in solving problems indicates, the bonds between friends and family are very tight in Brazil. Children usually live with their parents at least until they are married. If they do not earn enough to start on their own, married children will continue to stay in their family home. Children who move out usually remain close to home and visit their parents frequently.

A mother washes the clothes while her toddler is all soaped up and ready for a bath.

Brazil has a social security system, but most of the elderly still depend on their offspring to support them. Popular wisdom regards lots of children as the best insurance against hardship in old age. For the poor, unfortunately, neither plan works. Unable to support all their children, many poor parents have no choice but to send them into the streets to find work. Brazil's cultural emphasis on family unity makes its problem with homeless children all the more tragic.

Brazilians also stay in touch with relatives beyond their immediate family. Most young Americans have never met their second cousins. In Brazil, such distant cousins often see each other.

Godparents are very important in Brazil too. A man who agrees to sponsor a child at baptism becomes a *padrinho* to the child, and a *compadre* to the child's parents. The first word translates as "little father," the second could be interpreted as "joint father." A godparent and his family become accepted members of the family of the baptized child, just as if they had married into the family.

Brazilians are a people who treasure friendships.

FRIENDSHIP

Brazilians have two kinds of friends: social and close friends. Social friends are people you get together with to eat, dance or discuss local news, but not to touch on intimate subjects like family problems or personal ambitions. Nor will they meet in each other's homes; this is a private place reserved for family and close friends.

Only after many years will two Brazilians become close friends. The understanding and loyalty characterizing this degree of friendship takes long to evolve. Most have only a handful, whom they call *compadres*. These friends are accepted as family and can be counted on in any crisis.

Duty demands that relatives and friends help each other when a need arises, even if it involves hardship. A city-dweller would be bound to provide lodging to a visiting distant cousin, regardless of how long he or she might stay. Were he to suggest that the relative leave, or even help pay for rent or food, he would be considered rude and ungrateful. A good family man would refuse to accept contributions from a visiting relative; to do so would be to admit that he could not fulfill his duty. Modern economics and values are gradually changing this.

A Brazilian family of Japanese ancestry and their guests share drinks, laughs, and a plate of crabs.

THE GATHERING OF FRIENDS

Brazilians love to be around other people. They enjoy chatting or dancing late into the night with friends. They love to have relatives and *compadres* stop by their homes.

A long period of drinking and conversation will precede the meal when Brazilians hold a dinner party. Often, the host will not seat guests until 11 at night. At no time will the host leave guests to attend to the preparation of the meal. To do so would be seen as lacking respect, a sign of inadequate preparation for their arrival. If possible, servants will be employed to prepare the meal; if not, all details will be taken care of in advance. A guest may bring a gift of flowers, but would never bring a food dish. This would be seen as an insulting suggestion that the host needs help to entertain friends.

Because of the privacy of the home, most large parties take place in

clubs or community halls. Even parties for teenagers will start late, often after 10 p.m., and continue until the early morning hours.

Food, music and dancing are standard ingredients of these festivities. Guests are not restricted to those with invitations. Brazilians think nothing of bringing a friend or visiting relative with them to the event. Strangers should not expect to be introduced to other party-goers, however. Formal introductions are considered too stiff for the festive atmosphere—you don't need to know someone's name in order to have a good conversation and a good time.

For both business and social events, Brazilians habitually show up late. Anyone arriving at the party less than half an hour after the time on the invitation is most likely to find an empty room, and may even have arrived before the hosts. For the rare event in which guests are expected to arrive on time, invitations specify the beginning hour as Swiss Time, British Time or American Time.

Most parties are held in community halls or country clubs like this one in Rio de Janeiro.

On her 15th birthday, a Brazilian ceases to be a girl and begins to receive the treatment of a woman.

BIRTHDAYS Children's birthdays in Brazil are similar to those in the United States. Adults often have small family gatherings, followed by larger parties to celebrate. Even casual friends will make every effort to attend. To miss such an event would be to fail in one's duty as a friend.

Upper-class families mark the 15th birthday of a daughter with a big debutante ball. The birthday girl and her closest friends dress in white gowns; their escorts wear suits or tuxedos. The evening often begins with a Mass, then guests attend a reception where a lavish buffet and live band await. At midnight, the guest of honor formally "enters" society by having one dance with her father, followed by a second with her escort.

WEDDINGS Before the wedding, the groom and his friends celebrate with a bachelor party at a club, while the bridesmaids give a bridal shower in the kitchen of the bride's best friend.

The immediate family will attend a small ceremony where civil documents are signed, but the big event is the church wedding. All relatives and family friends will attend the Mass and the large reception which follows. After cutting their wedding cake and bidding farewell to the guests, the newlyweds will leave on their honeymoon.

FUNERALS Families usually bury their dead within 24 hours. News of the funeral travels by word of mouth, and those notified are expected to attend. The body lies in state in a coffin at the family home, dressed in black. Mourners will drink and trade stories about the deceased throughout the night. At a designated time, a hearse carrying the coffin leads a procession to a church, where a requiem is offered. In smaller towns, the body will be buried in the church's private cemetery; in large cities, the procession moves to a larger public cemetery. Masses are held in memory of the deceased after 7 days, 30 days, and a year.

The gauchos, proud and absolutely die-hard, are the frontrunners of the Brazilian machismo attitude.

THE MACHO MEN

Despite changing social trends, Brazil remains very much a man's country. The husband traditionally earns and manages his family's income, while the wife does the daily house chores and raises the children.

As in most South American countries, the Brazilian man always takes the lead in courting women. A woman who displays too much initiative in approaching men quickly gains a bad reputation. Men are expected to aggressively pursue women.

A strict code of chivalry moderates this pursuit. Men are expected to give up their seats on buses and to open doors for women. In a restaurant, a man will seat his date, order for her, and pay the bill. Such small courtesies are important to a man, since they establish him as a protector of women. The desire to play a leading role and to uphold one's honor constitute the two main features of male machismo. Brazilian men also do not feel compelled to act tough or hide their emotions. They do not hesitate to show affection to women, to hug *compadres* or to cry over dying relatives.

THE GIRLS FROM IPANEMA

Brazilian women are famous around the world for their beauty and charm. "The Girl From Ipanema," made famous by a popular song of the 1960s, has become an icon for Latin beauty.

Enchanted by a typical Brazilian beauty that frequented Rio de Janeiro's most famous beach, songwriter Tom Jobim and a friend put their feelings into music and came up with a song that became a standard.

Typical Brazilian grace, charm and beauty.

Looking good is very important to Brazilian women, who seek to exude style and charm in all they do. They like to dress fashionably, always wearing fancier clothing than their male companions.

Girls learn to wear jewelry and apply make-up at an early age. On the beach, they wear bathing suits that not only help them have a good tan but also encourage them to keep trim.

While machismo propels a man to play a dominating role, Brazilian feminity promotes dependency on others. Marriage is deemed essential for feminine self-fulfillment, to the point that neighbors will pity single women who are in their 30s.

Men like to feel that they are in control, but Brazilian women are experts at manipulating male egos with their twinkling eyes and gracious smiles.

Polite interaction between the sexes often plays out like a game. Men lavish attention on women, often leading up to romantic propositions. The women will smile at their suitors, chat with them and appreciate their attention. But rarely, if ever, will they yield to an advance.

The flirting sometimes crosses a fine line and fuels masculine jealousy, exposing a double standard in the Brazilian attitude toward marriage. Society, and women, quietly tolerate extramarital affairs by husbands—many even accept these as the inevitable result of machismo. But each year, hundreds of wives are beaten, and even killed, because of the jealousy and suspicions of their husbands. Women rarely report these, since the law rarely punishes men for these "crimes of passion."

This is slowly changing. Brazil is gradually overturning such attitudes. Stricter laws have been passed against these crimes. An increasing number of women are taking on careers and participating in activities previously regarded as un-feminine, such as team sports and politics. After the 1986 election, the number of women in the Federal Chamber of Deputies jumped from eight to 26.

But Brazilian society still has a long way to go in breaking male dominance. Consider the political ties of nine of these deputies: two are daughters of former presidents, four are wives of senators, two are spouses of former state governors, and one is the widow of an important city mayor. Unfortunately, the "old boy" network is still alive, and still the most effective way to get things done in Brazil.

BRINGING UP CHILDREN

Brazilian parents readily admit that their children are spoiled. Because of large families and frequent visits by relatives, children are never left alone. Many families hire nurses to look after the children, and those who cannot afford them can count on help from relatives.

Babies in particular receive constant attention. They rarely escape the hands of the caretaker, and when they cry they become the center of all attention. Strangers on streets will stop to offer suggestions to a mother with a crying infant.

Junior takes the plunge in his miniature bathtub while his siblings keep a watchful eye.

Few parents believe in strict discipline. Children who behave inappropriately around guests will be sent out of the room. But if they act up in church or in a store, they are usually ignored. They believe it is unavoidable that children will be bored or unhappy in a place where there is nothing to entertain them.

Until they become teenagers, children rarely do chores. No upper-class Brazilian allows his children to work part-time while attending school. They feel such work suggests that the family is in financial trouble.

In this male-oriented society, boys are treated more leniently than girls. Daughters usually cannot stay out late, and parents take a keener interest in their friends.

Dating usually begins around the age of 17. The first dates come from a familiar circle of friends, and are not seen as anything serious. Groups of couples go out together—parents don't like daughters going out without a chaperone.

The first sign that a relationship is serious comes when the boy is invited to his girlfriend's home.

EDUCATION

Every January, thousands of 18-year-olds crowd into lecture halls, gymnasiums, and even soccer stadiums to take the *vestibular*, the examination which determines whether they will be admitted into a university.

Fifty years ago, Brazilians considered education a privilege of the rich. Wealthy parents sent their children to Europe to learn about correct social etiquette and classical civilizations.

Today, the number of children in school is almost six times greater than in 1950.

Uniformed schoolchildren in the hot sun in João Pessoa.

Students attend eight years of elementary school and three years of high school. Because so many teenagers work and because of a shortage of classroom space, many high schools hold classes in shifts. Progress is measured in classroom hours rather than school years, so that working students can move at their own pace.

Public and private universities each give different exams, with a different exam to be taken to enter each school in the university. Students who want to study nutrition or biology must take two different exams; if they want to apply to two private and a public institution, they have to take six exams. Once admitted as biology students, they cannot switch to nutrition without taking the *vestibular* again.

Tuition is very low for those who pass, thanks to support from the government. University students are a select group: only one in 100 children who enroll in the first grade ever sets foot inside a university.

RELIGION

NINE OUT OF TEN Brazilians say they are Roman Catholics, making Brazil the world's largest Catholic nation. But the pope may have a hard time recognizing some of the practices of Brazilian Catholics.

On New Year's Eve in Rio de Janeiro, women dressed in white march across the beach and into the sea, carrying a statue of the Virgin Mary. They launch miniature boats carrying flowers and perfume. If the boats make it out to sea, it means that their offerings have been accepted by the Virgin Mary. If they wash to shore, then they have been rejected.

On the third Thursday of January in Salvador da Bahia, colorfully dressed women scrub the steps leading to the Church of Nosso Senhor do Bonfim—literally, Our Lord of the Good Ending. In the "miracle room" of this church, hundreds of wax models of human limbs hang, left behind as tokens of thanks by the faithful who believe Nosso Senhor do Bonfim healed them.

In October in Belem, thousands join a procession leading a statue of Our Lady of Nazareth through the city streets. They grab hold of a thick rope several blocks long, which is used to pull the carriage bearing the statue. They believe that she will answer the prayers of those who help her pass along the streets.

That same month, back in Rio de Janeiro, thousands of faithful get down on their knees and climb the 365 steps leading up to the Church of Our Lady of the Cliff. They do so either to atone for their sins, or to express gratitude.

Opposite: **A young *baiana* carries a flower vase on her head in a *macumba* procession. *Macumba* is an African-Brazilian religion that is often compared with the voodoo cults of the Caribbean.**

Below: **The interior of Brasília's magnificent cathedral.**

FOLK RELIGION

Each of the previously mentioned ceremonies shows the influence of African and, to a lesser extent, native Indian religions. The New Year's Eve festival is dedicated not to the Virgin Mary, but to Iemanja, an African goddess of the sea. Missionaries started Belem's annual procession in 1763 as a tool to attract Amazon Indians to Christianity.

Macumba **rituals with their trademark street-side offerings, colorful mats and candles.**

Catholic priests arrived in Brazil with the early colonizers and set out to convert the Indians and later the African slaves. They achieved partial success: their pupils became Catholics in name, but molded their new religion to fit old spiritual practices. The missionaries could do little about it because of their small numbers. To this day, Brazil suffers from a shortage of priests. In 1970, the Church estimated it had only one priest for every 6,000 Catholics.

This shortage has always been acute among the poor. Left to their own devices, they developed their own form of folk Catholicism. They adopted some elements of Indian religion, such as resorting to medicine men to heal sicknesses, and some elements of European folklore, such as a belief in wolfmen.

The African religions were the most influential of all. Brazilians took on African gods called *orixás* and gave them Christian names. Oxala became Jesus Christ—popularly known as Nosso Senhor do Bonfim. Ogun, a hunter god, and Xango, a god of lightning, took on the identities of Saints Anthony and George. Iemanja is, as we have seen, portrayed as the Virgin Mary. Saints Jerome, Cosmos and Damian, Barbara, Anna and many others inherited the identities of African *orixás*.

The Catholic faithful carrying a statue of a patron saint in Brazil's northeast. Brazil's Catholics do not hesitate to kneel and worship at the altars of other gods.

To the faithful, these saints are just as important as Jesus Christ or the Virgin Mary. The main concern of many Brazilians is not so much salvation or life after death, but surviving in this world. They pray to the saints, whom they believe are capable of bestowing favors upon those who revere them. St. Anthony can help single women find husbands; St. Blas protects against sore throats; St. Lucia can heal the blind.

To win a saint's favor, believers make promises. They may promise to climb the steps of a church on their knees or wash it. If a saint cures them of an affliction, they may make a pilgrimage to that saint's shrine to offer a model of their healed limb or organ. In larger cities, processions honoring different saints are common. Every town organizes a procession on the feast day of its patron saint. One survey showed that the Brazilian Catholic Church organizes more than 37,000 processions annually—a rate of over 100 each day!

Nowadays, it is impossible to distinguish between "real" Catholics and "folk" Catholics. Every Brazilian Catholic accepts some folk belief. In general, however, it follows economic lines: the upper class adheres more to traditional Catholic beliefs than the poor, with the middle class somewhere in between.

THE CHURCH'S SOCIAL ROLE

While they have always been few in number, Catholic priests have played an important role throughout Brazil's history in working for the social well-being of the masses.

Jesuit priests arrived with the earliest colonizers and provided education for both the settlers and the Indians. They also fought vigorously to protect the Indians from slavery, until their efforts caused the Portuguese king to expel them from Brazil in 1759.

During the colonial period, priests began to establish lay brotherhoods, some of which still exist today. These organizations played the role of a social security agency. They provided help for elderly or sick members, and built numerous hospitals, orphanages and churches.

Today, Brazilian priests have taken a leading role in pushing for aid to native Indians, landless peasants and the poor. The National Council of Brazilian Bishops has said that the Church should not support political parties, but it should strive to promote the fair use of land and the fair treatment of workers.

Radical priests accept the doctrine of "liberation theology," which combines Marxism and Christianity. They believe that a struggle by the poor working class is needed to carry out God's plan. Liberation theology shows the extremes to which some priests have taken their role as agents of social change.

AFRICAN RELIGIONS

African rituals still thrive in Brazil, particularly among the poor. Carried out secretly at night in special ceremonial houses, they play a part in preserving the African heritage of Brazil's blacks. The priest or priestess who directs these rites can often tell the story of his or her ancestors, going back to the time when they left Africa in slave ships.

But like Brazilian Catholicism, these African religions are no longer "pure." They too have been influenced by European and Indian practices. Many non-blacks have been accepted as members of these cults. Social status is more of an issue than is race for membership. If active members should earn enough to rise into the middle or upper class, their new social position will probably force them to quit participation.

Cults introduced from West Africa are the roots from which most Brazilian rituals evolved. In Africa, these cults centered around the ceremonial preparation of an object known as a "fetish," which supposedly held supernatural powers. In Brazil, the fetish has given way to the powers of the *orixás*, or gods. A pantheon of *orixás* existed in Africa, but took on a larger role in Brazil due to the influence of Catholic teachings.

Candomblé and *macumba*, the two main cults, reflect the varying degrees of outside influence on African religions. *Candomblé*, practiced mainly in Salvador da Bahia, has stayed closer to its West African roots. *Macumba*, practiced mostly in Rio de Janeiro, brings beliefs from West and South Africa together with European beliefs.

Hundreds of colorfully decorated boats and ships accompany thousands of people on shore escorting a statue of Jesus during the celebration of the feast of Lord Jesus of the Navigators. This event has most of the coastal northeast joining Salvador in celebration.

CANDOMBLE A *pai de santo* (father of the saint) or *mai de santo* (mother of the saint) presides over *candomblé* rituals—both men and women are able to serve. The inner circle of devotees are the *filhos de santo* (children of the saint). In Bahia, these are usually young women who undergo a complicated initiation ritual to reach this stage.

For a period of up to one year, they must remain inside the ceremonial house of their *pai de santo*, eating a set diet and observing a strict set of rules. When this is completed, they are bathed in water spiced with scented leaves, after which the blood of a sacrificed animal is poured over their head.

The main *candomblé* ritual is the giving of a "meal" to the *orixás*. On set dates, the *pai de santo* prepares a fetish for a designated god. The fetish for each *orixá* must be prepared differently. For Xango, whose fetish is a stone, he will place the stone in a basin, surround it with palm

Candomblé believers link hands while still in a trance during a beach ceremony in Rio de Janeiro.

oil and sacred leaves, then spill the blood of a sacrificed rooster over it. The *pai de santo* places the fetish in a special worship room. Followers crowd around the room, with one side reserved for a band of drummers. The *pai de santo* stands in the center, surrounded by the *filhos de santo*.

Several small initial offerings are made to different *orixás*, always starting with the evil spirit named Exu. It is believed that an early gift to this god prevents his interference in later offerings.

Accompanied by the thumping of the drums, the *filhos de santo* dance and sing invocations to different *orixás*. Hours pass, the rhythm of the drumbeat gets faster, the dancing becomes more frenzied and emotions build up. The climax comes when an *orixá* possesses the spirit of one of the dancers. The entranced *filho de santo* begins to shake uncontrollably until she collapses. When she revives, the *pai de santo* gives her the symbol of the *orixá* who had visited her soul, and she continues to dance. Those present revere the *orixá* in her, and ask favors of it. During the ceremony, which may last all night, several *orixás* will make their presence known.

Candomblé priests and priestesses presiding over a ceremony. Leading *candomblé* priestesses are said to be able to tell the names of their ancestors, going as far back as when their ancestors were still in Africa. Before these priestesses die, they pass on their knowledge to their understudies, who will memorize by heart the entire family tree.

Bahian women and girls take a breather after an exhausting *macumba* ceremony.

MACUMBA Followers of *macumba* appeal to a wider array of spirits. This cult combines elements of *candomblé* with the ancestral worship brought to Brazil by slaves from the south of Africa, and with the European philosophy of spiritualism. According to this philosophy, the living can communicate with the souls of the dead.

The *macumba* and *candomblé* rites are similar, but the spirits that possess *macumba* dancers are not always *orixás*. They may represent a natural force, some god, or an ancestor of one of the followers. The spirits sometimes speak to those present through the voice of the possessed *filho de santo*. Just as often, the fun-loving spirits just want to use their hosts as means to drink, dance, smoke and have a good time.

Special *macumba* ceremonies focus only on healing. In these, only the *pai de santo* becomes entranced. Possessed by the appropriate spirit, he can supposedly cure afflictions by simply blowing cigar smoke over his patient or by brushing feathers over the wounded area.

RURAL MIRACLE WORKERS

A different type of religion flourishes in the harsh conditions of Brazil's northeast. Dry weather makes life difficult for the farmers in this region, so they are understandably drawn to preachers who herald the end of this world and the beginning of a new, more just society.

Over the years, many such ministers have won the reputation of being miracle workers. The two most famous drew large numbers of followers in the late 19th century.

ANTONIO CONSELHEIRO Antonio Maciel, who became known as Antonio Conselheiro (meaning Antonio the Counselor), began preaching in the 1870s. He believed that the world would come to an end by 1899, when King Sebastian would appear in Brazil to bring justice to all. This 16th century Portuguese king had disappeared during a holy crusade to North Africa, and many people at that time regarded him as a savior who would re-appear to end injustice.

Conselheiro gained a reputation as a miracle worker and soon found himself thronged by followers. He also found himself in trouble when the army overthrew Dom Pedro II in 1889.

Brazil's new government did not like him, since he had always taught that an emperor ruled by divine right. The army sent four expeditions against New Jerusalem, the city Conselheiro had built in Bahia as his base. The first three failed, but the fourth, in 1897, destroyed the town and its leader. According to legend, only a child, an old man and two wounded men survived. The world did end for Conselheiro and his followers, but myths about him live on in the northeast today.

FATHER CICERO A contemporary of Conselheiro, he fared better. Father Cicero, a priest from the state of Ceara, survives today as a religious icon and as an object of worship.

He first became popular because of his compassion for the poor. But he became famous in 1890 because of the "miracle of the host." During a Mass that year, a woman who received Holy Communion from him immediately collapsed to the floor with blood dripping from her mouth. Believers claimed the host had miraculously turned into the blood of Jesus Christ.

Skeptics claimed that sickness made the woman cough up blood, so the local bishop sent in investigators. His team concluded that no miracle had taken place, and the Church eventually excommunicated Father Cicero. These actions did not hurt his popularity.

The people of the northeast believed the priest had magical powers. They saved everything he touched, from his clipped fingernails to the water he used to wash his clothes. When Father Cicero died in 1934, he was one of the most influential men in Brazil.

He is still worshiped today. A 75-foot statue of him stands in the town of Juazeiro do Norte, where thousands arrive each year to visit his grave. Shops all over the northeast sell images of Father Cicero, and many Brazilians pray to him for favors. Some believe he has not died, but will return soon to herald the coming of a new age.

Opposite: **The giant statue of Father Cicero in Juazeiro do Norte. Cicero was considered a sort of savior who would one day magically make the dry lands of the northeast flourish like beautiful gardens and stop poverty and hunger.**

LANGUAGE

BRAZILIANS ARE THE ONLY LATIN AMERICANS who speak Portuguese. Along with all the other countries of North and South America, they inherited their language from European colonizers.

As the English spoken in the United States differs in some ways from that in England, so has Brazil's Portuguese developed a character of its own. Educated citizens of Brazil and Portugal can still communicate once they adjust to each other's accents. Working class Brazilians, however, would have a hard time understanding their European cousins.

The difference between the two stems mostly from the influence of Brazil's Indians. The early colonists survived by trading with these Indians, so they had to learn to communicate with them. For the first 200 years of Brazil's history, they used an Indian language called *Tupi-Guarani* more than Portuguese.

Today, *Tupi-Guarani* survives only among a few Indian tribes living near the border with Paraguay, but it left its mark on Brazilian Portuguese. One researcher compiled a list of 20,000 Portuguese words with Indian origins, about a sixth of the total Portuguese vocabulary. Portuguese settlers borrowed most of these words to name unfamiliar animals and plants. Some of the names, such as *manioc* and *jaguar*, have even found their way into the English language.

Other outside influences have flavored Brazil's Portuguese. In Bahia and Rio de Janeiro, Brazilians speak with a flowing, almost musical rhythm. Many attribute this to the African heritage of those states. The vocabulary and cadence in some southern towns, in turn, reflect the influence of German, Italian and Spanish immigrants.

Opposite: **Brazilian newspapers on display. English-language papers such as the *Wall Street Journal* and the *Miami Herald* are also sold in Brazil.**

ALPHABETS AND ACCENTS

The Portuguese alphabet has three fewer letters than the English alphabet. The letters "k," "w" and "y" appear only in foreign names used by Brazilians.

The pronunciation of the other 23 letters is similar to English, except for the letter "x," which sounds like "sh." For example, "Xingu" is pronounced "Shingu."

As in English, "c" can have a hard or soft sound. When it is annotated with a cedilla, appearing as "ç," it is always pronounced softly. For example, "açucar," meaning sugar, sounds like "ah-sue-kahr."

A Txukarramai Indian chief discussing land problems with a settler.

Three accent marks appear in Portuguese words: the circumflex (ˆ), the acute (ˊ) and the tilde (~). The first two indicate syllables to be stressed; the tilde gives a vowel a nasal sound similar to the vowel sound in the English word "ounce."

Unaccented Portuguese words are usually stressed on the starting syllable if they end in "a," "e" or "o" sounds. Otherwise, the accent falls on the final syllable. For example, "casa" (house) is pronounced "KAH-zah," while "casar" (to marry) is pronounced "kah-ZAHR."

NAMES

In general, Brazilians are warm, friendly and love good conversation in a cheerful atmosphere. At the same time, they are very aware of the perks of social standing, and are careful to show proper respect at all times with people they talk to. The manner in which they address one another reflects both the formal and informal sides of their personalities.

FORMAL NAMES Brazilians only use "you" when speaking to close friends, children and those from the lower classes. Any casual acquaintance, senior citizen, or stranger is addressed as "o senhor" (the gentleman) or "a senhora" (the lady). Instead of asking "How are you today?" they would ask "How is the lady today?"

Brazilians often bestow further honorary titles on wealthier or better-educated citizens. Just because someone is called Colonel da Silva doesn't necessarily mean he is a military officer. Likewise, Doctor da Silva may not be a physician, just a prosperous merchant who knows how to read and conjugate verbs in the subjunctive tense. This is particularly true in rural towns where most people are illiterate. Those who can decipher official documents are guaranteed a place of honor in the community.

School time: A Guajajara child getting down to some serious business with her schoolwork.

COUNTING TO TEN THE INDIAN WAY

When the Portuguese first arrived in Brazil, they found Indians speaking a number of different languages. Today, just a few of these dialects survive. If Brazilian children spoke the language of the Cayapo Indians who live in the Xingu National Park, they would count to 10 like this:

 1 pudi
 2 amaikrut
 3 amaikrutikeke
 4 amaikrutamaikrut
 5 amaikrutamaikrutikeke
 6 amaikrutamaikrutamaikrut
 7 amaikrutamaikrutamaikrutikeke
 8 amaikrutamaikrutamaikrutamaikrut
 9 amaikrutamaikrutamaikrutamaikrutikeke
10 amaikrutamaikrutamaikrutamaikrutamaikrut

INFORMAL NAMES In general, knowing someone's name is not as important as it is in the United States or Europe. Often, introductions will not be made when a Brazilian brings a friend to a party—to do so would add an air of formality to a friendly setting. If an introduction is made, only the first name or a nickname will be given.

Another reason for this is that often a Brazilian will not know the last name of his friends. Most Brazilians are known by either their first or last name, not by both. A teacher named Carlos Mattos would be called Professor Carlos by his students and Senhor Carlos by his colleagues. His close friends would simply call him Carlos, but many of them would not know his last name.

Brazilians often use names which appear nowhere on their birth certificates. Adults often christen young children with nicknames that last for a lifetime. Brazil's most famous soccer player, Edson Arantes de Nascimento, is know to his countrymen and to the world as Pelé. Two top players on Brazil's 1990 World Cup soccer team go by the names

Careca (meaning "bald man") and Alemão ("German"). This practice is not just limited to sports stars.

Brazilians know Luis Inacio da Silva, the leader of the Worker's Party and the runner-up in the 1989 presidential elections, as Lula. Brazilian children know the folk story about Lampeão, a famous bandit of the northeast. But few children recognize him by his full name, Virgulino Ferreira. Brazil's most famous sculptor is known as Aleijadinho, which means "the little cripple" (see page 90).

BODY LANGUAGE

Actions speak louder than words when Brazilians greet one another. For a business contact or a new acquaintance, a handshake will do, perhaps accompanied by a slap on the back if the setting is informal.

But a meeting of friends calls for something more. Two men exchange an *abraço*, a firm hug, while women trade *beijinhos*, kisses on the cheek. By custom, a married woman receives a kiss on each side of the face, but a single woman gets an extra kiss. If it doesn't come, she's liable to say: "Give me three so that I won't be an old maid!" When men and women meet they are slightly more restrained, but relatives and friends will still trade one or two *beijinhos*.

As this custom shows, touching people is more common in Brazil than in the United States. Foreigners often feel uncomfortable about how close Brazilians will stand during a conversation, and about the way they might grab their arm or touch them to emphasize a point.

Brazilians, in turn, don't understand why Americans, for example, will excuse themselves when they need to squeeze out of a crowd. In their view, brushing by a body to get out of an elevator, or even using hands to gently move people to the side, requires no apology or excuse.

Yanomami Indians in an invitation talk. The messenger of the guest party embraces the headman of the host party.

GESTURES: USING THE HANDS

Brazilians are uninhibited when they talk. Good conversation means loud voices and lots of hand movement. To them, anyone who debates with a level voice and his hands at his side doesn't really believe what he is saying. Here is a sampling of a wide array of gestures.

(Figure A)

One of the most common gestures is to make a snapping noise with the hand. Holding thumb and middle finger together, a person will relax her hand and shake it so that the index finger whips against the middle finger. Brazilian children learn this at an early age, but foreigners have a hard time picking it up. People snap their fingers so often it's impossible to assign a precise meaning to the gesture. A Brazilian snaps to indicate pain, to tell his friends to hurry up, to show appreciation for a joke. If a child disobeys his parents, his friends snap their fingers as if to say: "Boy, are you in trouble now!"

(Figure B)

Another versatile gesture is shaking your hands back and forth, so that the fingertips of each hand brush against one another (Figure A). Usually, this is to say, "I don't care" or "It doesn't matter." Asked how he is doing, a bored man may shrug his shoulders and respond with this gesture to indicate that things are as usual, not too good, not too bad.

"Everything's great!" This is shown by holding five fingers up to one's mouth, kissing them, then opening up the hands as you fling it forward (Figure B). This gesture is also used to show appreciation for a beautiful painting or a beautiful woman.

If Americans don't believe something, they sometimes exclaim "My eye!" Brazilians point to their eye with a knowing grin and pull down the skin beneath the eye (Figure C). They might emphasize the point by saying, *Aqui, oh!* meaning "Sure, right here!"

"I can't take it any more!" Holding the fingers together with hands pointing upward means you've had enough (Figure D). A Brazilian will also use this gesture when talking about a crowded place.

Brazilians call a miser a *pão duro*, meaning a hard piece of bread. To accuse someone of being stingy without saying anything, they show a clenched fist.

"Let's have a drink." Brazilians might hold their thumb and index finger together to their mouth, and go through the motion of drinking from a cup.

To show approval or to indicate that everything is all right, Brazilians use the thumbs-up gesture.

(Figure C)

(Figure D)

THE ARTS

MORE THAN ANY OTHER ART FORM, Brazil's music best captures the nation's heritage. Brazilian music developed from the blending of European, African and native Indian roots.

The first Jesuit missionaries to Brazil discovered that ritual chanting accompanied by rattles and pan pipes played a key role in the religious rites of the native Indians. These missionaries then taught the Indians the Catholic Mass using Gregorian chants. This Indian tradition still survives in the *caboclinho*, a folk dance of Brazil's northeast. Dressed in Indian costumes, the entourage marches in two columns. A chief recites passages, finishing each line on a low note, and the other dancers respond with a set chorus. A three-man band accompanies the entourage, playing the flute, *reco-reco* and drum. Each man reinforces the beat by using his bow and arrow as rhythm sticks.

Music and dancing also played an essential role in the rites of the African slaves. The colonists considered the slaves' dances wild and obscene, and for some time tried to suppress them. At the same time, plantation owners appreciated the musical skills of their slaves and taught them to play European instruments. Bands made up of slaves provided the music when owners entertained. Gradually, African rhythms and instruments found their way into the mainstream. By the early 1800s, colonial barons and ladies in elegant salons found themselves dancing the *lundu*, still defined by the dictionary as a "primitive, lascivious dance." Today's samba is a direct descendant of the *lundu*.

At the same time, the slaves learned to appreciate European instruments like the accordion, tambourine, guitar and various others that still form the backbone of Brazil's music. The Africans adapted these to their style, and incorporated some of the European beats and harmonies.

Opposite: **Manaus' Opera House was built in 1896 with material from France and Scotland, while parts of it were painted by a famous Italian artist. The project cost $10 million.**

One old cliché is that Brazil is a country of rhythm. What it really has are many rhythms. Brazil is still one of the best places in the world for grassroots ethnic music.

The *surdo*, a favorite musical instrument of the national beat.

THE NATIONAL BEAT

Today, just as European, African and Indian blood have mixed to produce countless ethnic variations in Brazil, so have they combined to produce an incredible array of music and dance styles.

Just as a catalog of names exists to describe different groups of Brazilians, so have Brazil's musicians many names to define their art. The most famous is the samba.

Samba is the national beat, but there are many different types of samba. *Samba do morro* (hill samba) refers to samba played by a large group using only percussion instruments.

In Carnival parades, the samba schools play *samba enredo* (theme samba), with a lead singer and a chorus accompanying the percussion band. Small groups in nightclubs perform *samba canção* (samba song) or *samba de salão* (parlor samba). To a samba beat, their lead vocalist may croon a romantic song of love, or make a sarcastic commentary on local politics.

Samba de roda (circle samba) refers to the traditional slave dance, where participants sit in a circle with one person in the middle. When he has finished his turn, he would designate the next dancer by standing in front of that person and thrusting his hips forward.

In a *samba rural* (also called *samba paulista*), dancers line up in two files, while in a *samba lençol* (sheet samba), couples dance in step.

As with ethnic descriptions, most Brazilians have little time for detailed musical terminology. Whether the sound comes from a costumed percussion section parading along the street, or from a lone guitar player accompanied by a friend drumming his hands on a table, a Brazilian need only hear it to know that it is samba music.

BUMBA-MEU-BOI

Portuguese colonists brought several dramatic folk dances to Brazil, called *folguedos*. Usually performed during religious festivals, many survive to this day. The *congada* re-enacts a battle of the Crusades between Christians and Moors, while the *cavalhada* mimics a medieval jousting competition.

The most common surviving dance, the *bumba-meu-boi*, has become very Brazilian. Folk groups around the country perform it during the Christmas season. The dance centers on the death and resurrection of a bull. Some consider it a parody of a bullfight, while others believe its origin lies in the rites of pagan religions which considered the bull a symbol of power and fertility.

The plot usually has a cowboy named Mateus trying to sell a bull to a wealthy rancher. The bull attacks the crowd which surrounds it, is stabbed with a knife and dies. Mateus, however, revives it using folk medicine.

Brazilians today don't really care much about the story or its symbolism. The *bumba-meu-boi* is now mainly a festive occasion, filled with bright costumes, lively music and dancing. Witty exchanges between the solo singers and the chorus add elements of humor and social commentary.

The star of the dance is the bull. One man plays the part, bearing on his shoulders a bull-shaped wooden framework covered with velvet. Authentic bullhorns, elegant stitching, ribbons, and sometimes even colorful semi-precious stones decorate the cloth.

Always the center of attention, the bull attacks then retreats, shudders in the throes of death, then bounces back to life. In the end, he breaks out of the circle of dancers and leads a festive procession through the streets.

The Bumba-Meu-Boi is generally seen as the comic representation of Portugal's non-lethal bullfights. This very rhythmic and colorful dance is performed most authentically in the northeastern states.

MUSICAL INSTRUMENTS

EUROPEAN INSTRUMENTS   The Portuguese contributed an array of stringed instruments to Brazil's music. The Portuguese guitar, the *viola*, was the favorite tool of Iberian troubadours as far back as the 13th century. This 10-string instrument is gradually giving way to the modern six-string guitar, but it is still an essential part of Brazilian folk music. The *cavaquinho* (a small guitar similar to a Hawaiian ukelele), the *bandolim* (mandolin), and the *rabeca* (a Portuguese fiddle) live on as well. Virtuoso performers on these instruments come together to play a lively acoustic style Brazilians call *choro* music.

The accordian, tambourine and the triangle all came to Brazil from Europe. So did the *tarol* and the *surdo*: the former is a small drum similar to those used in marching bands, while the latter is a large bass drum.

AFRICAN INSTRUMENTS   Brazil inherited numerous instruments from Africa, the most unique being the *cuica*, which produces a squeal unlike anything produced by any other instrument. A narrow rod fastened to the middle of the drumhead extends through the hollow cylinder of the *cuica*. Musicians rub a damp cloth along this rod. The friction causes the leather skin to vibrate, creating a high-pitched sound, something like the noise a damp cloth makes when rubbed against a window. By pressing their fingers at different points along the drumhead and varying the speed with which they rub the rod, they can control the noise the *cuica* makes. The result is intriguing.

Another African import is the *tamborim*, a small drum the size of a tambourine that does not have the metal

Brazilian street musicians drum up a beat accompanied by the accordion and tambourine.

shingles and is not meant to be shaken. Samba masters usually hold it in one hand while drumming it with a small baton.

Another popular instrument is the *reco-reco*. Brazilians use this word to describe a frog's croak. They scrape a stick along the carved notches of the wooden instrument to produce a similar sound.

The *berimbau* also emits a unique sound. With one wire tied between the ends of a slightly curved stick, it looks like an archer's bow. Master players twang the wire by hitting it with a stick. They vary the note by using their free hand to tighten or loosen the wire. A gourd attached at the bottom of the *berimbau* acts as a resonator. The musician holds it against his stomach to start, then changes the timbre of the sound by moving it to and from his body. The *berimbau* is today used exclusively to accompany *capoeira,* an African martial arts dance. The mysterious twang of the instrument provides a perfect backdrop for the exotic leaps and kicks of the *capoeira* dancers.

INDIAN INSTRUMENTS Rattles and pipes were the preferred instruments of Brazil's Indians. Some Indian tribes in the Amazon still bring out the *urua* for formal ceremonies. It takes a barrel-chested Indian with above-average lung capacity to blow music out of this 10-foot long pipe. Simpler and more common is the *pife*, a simple bamboo flute still popular among the poor in the north and northeast.

The standard Indian rattle is the *maraca*, a hollow gourd with a wooden handle partially filled with dried seeds. Africans also brought rattles with them to the new world, so scholars can only guess the origin of the several varieties used in Brazil.

Iaualapiti Indians in a festival playing their sacred flutes. Their music has little melody but complex rhythms. And their musical heritage is substantial: Indian contributions to popular music include percussion instruments, the nasal tone in song, the one-word chorus and the ending of a verse on a lower note.

Art lovers viewing an exhibition on the Avenida Rio Branco, with the Municipal Theater in the background. Located in the area are two other impressive buildings: the National Library that plays host to neo-classic and new art; and the Museum of Fine Arts which displays the works of Brazil's greatest artists.

POPULAR ART

Popular art flourishes all over Brazil. It can be found in almost any Brazilian town every weekend of the year at an open-air *feira*, or market. In the rural towns of the interior, these fairs are big events where vendors sell everything from chickens and pots and pans to carved nativity sets and cotton blouses. In larger cities, the weekend fairs focus more on popular art than on the essentials of everyday life.

Much of the art found at these *feiras* is linked to popular beliefs. Wood carvings or ceramic statues of various Catholic saints are sold as icons for the home.

Good luck charms are another best seller. Silversmiths in Bahia shape tiny individual fruits, birds and fish. Clusters of these attached to a chain make a *balangandā*. Tradition holds that each item in the cluster represents an individual *candomblé* spirit, so that together the pieces have the power to ward evil spirits away from anyone who wears them.

Another charm is the *figa*, a model of a clenched fist where the thumb sticks out between the index and middle fingers. While the origin of this symbol is unknown, many Brazilians wear it to fend off the "evil eye." Artisans at the *feiras* sell them in all sizes made out of wood, silver or semi-precious stones.

Away from the street markets, many artists run shops near churches dedicated to popular saints. They specialize in creating *ex votos*, items which Catholics offer to repay a saint for a favor he has done for them.

The quality of these gifts varies greatly. A poor man who has recovered from a broken leg may order a simple clay model of that limb. A wealthier man who has survived a car accident might request an elaborate painting depicting the crash and the saint's miraculous intercession.

The *carranca*, a figure-head on boats of the São Francisco River. The river is said to have a history of evil spirits, including "the Water Bitch," "the Water Monster," and "the Backwoodsman of the Water," who have sunk many ships in the past. The *carrancas* are there to scare these monsters away.

Along the São Francisco River in the northeast, superstition created another form of popular art. One hundred years ago, a riverboat captain depended on a large figurehead on the bow of his vessel to repel evil spirits. Sculptors carved these figures, called *carrancas*, to look as menacing as possible. Half man and half beast, the *carrancas'* eyes glare and their mouths roar to reveal sharp teeth and red throats.

Today, the belief in the *carrancas'* mystical powers has faded, but the folk art still survives.

Right: **The Last Supper, sculpted by Aleijadinho and his students.**

Below: **Aleijadinho's Statue of Christ.**

THE LITTLE CRIPPLE

Brazil's most famous sculptor is one of the world's most remarkable artists. Antonio Francisco Lisboa, born around 1740, became known as Aleijadinho, the "little cripple."

An unknown disease, perhaps leprosy or arthritis, paralyzed his hands in his prime, but he tied a hammer and a chisel to his wrists and continued to work.

In this way, he managed to complete 12 remarkable life-size soapstone statues of Old Testament biblical prophets and the 66 woodcarvings which make up the Stations of the Cross. Both sets of works are found in the town of Congonhas do Campo near Belo Horizonte.

The illegitimate son of a Portuguese architect and a slave, he received no formal education during his 80 years, and he never set his eyes on the ocean. Yet his masterpieces are considered among the finest of baroque art anywhere in the world. He learned about the European baroque style from books and missionaries.

Along with his sculptures, Aleijadinho designed many beautiful

churches, each with trademark large, rounded bell towers, altars featuring ornate engravings, and reliefs of angels and saints extending out of ceilings. Several of these churches stand in various cities around the state of Minas Gerais.

One of them is the Our Lady of Mount Carmo Church, and another is the São Francisco Chapel. These two churches represent the best of baroque art in Brazil and are considered among the world's finest. Both of them are found in the town of Ouro Preto, which the United Nations declared to be a World Cultural Monument.

Two blocks from the São Francisco Chapel is the town's monument to Aleijadinho, with his remains buried beneath a marker in a museum church. Some of his wood and soapstone carvings, documents about his career, and the illustrated Bibles he used to study are also displayed in the galleries of the church.

Ouro Preto, Brazil's baroque art monument to the world.

BRASILIA'S ARCHITECTURE

Brasília, a planned city built from scratch to be Brazil's capital, might some day be another World Cultural Monument.

Just as Aleijadinho became a driving force behind the baroque architecture of the town of Ouro Preto, so another famous Brazilian architect is the mastermind of many of the modern ideas seen in the buildings of Brasília.

Oscar Niemeyer has designed buildings in France, Algeria, the United States and all over Brazil. In Brasília, he teamed up with noted city planner Lucio Costa and artist Roberto Burle-Marx to create his most famous works.

One word sums up Niemeyer's style: simplicity. Never curve a wall when a straight line will do. Never use bright paints or bricks when the natural color of marble or concrete is more effective.

The three principal government buildings which border Brasília's Plaza of the Three Powers exhibit his practical design. The twin towers of the National Congress dominate the square, with a concrete dome alongside one tower offsetting an inverted concrete dome next to the other.

The president's Planalto Palace and the Supreme Court flank the Congress building. Both are similar in design. A long walkway leads up to a large patio, which surrounds a square structure with glass façades on all sides.

Eight pairs of identical government ministry buildings line an esplanade leading up to the Plaza of the Three Powers. The closest ministry to the Plaza, however, has its own unique design. Called the Itamarati Palace, the Foreign Ministry is a glass box encased in a concrete cage sitting in the middle of a pool of water.

The structures may look stark, but when the red evening sun reflects off the glass of the Planalto Palace or the waters around the Itamarati Palace, Brasília takes on a unique beauty.

Statue honoring those who built Brasília.

The outline of Niemeyer's buildings against the bright sky of Brazil's Central Plateau reminds the people of the ultimate symbolism of this planned capital: an expression of their nation's desire to conquer its isolated interior regions.

Today, Niemeyer continues to be Brazil's premier architect. His most recent contribution is the famed Sambadrome, Rio's Carnival grandstand.

LEISURE

BRAZIL IS A BIG COUNTRY with a variety of people engaging in a variety of pastimes. At the risk of generalizing, one could reduce Brazilian leisure activity to the three "s's": soccer, samba and sand.

SOCCER IS KING

Brazilians joke that they save Sunday for two religious ceremonies: they go to church, and then they go to a soccer match.

No sport in the world brings out the frenzy that soccer draws in Brazil, mainly because no sport dominates a nation the way soccer dominates Brazil. Brazilian athletes have won medals in sports ranging from swimming to volleyball to track and field. But anytime you see Brazilian children playing on an open patch of ground, odds are they will be kicking a soccer ball. Scoring a goal in the World Cup, the world's soccer championship, is the dream of every Brazilian boy.

Brazilians call soccer *futebol*, a Portuguese pronunciation of the English word "football." Soccer came to Brazil from England about one hundred years ago, but Brazil has made itself the best in its adopted sport. Most people would agree that Brazilians not only improved the game, they perfected it.

The Brazilian style of play, with its superb dribbling, flamboyant showmanship, graceful playmaking and incredible goals has continued to delight the world. To Brazilians, the result of a match is not the only thing that matters; the way goals are scored and made are just as important. Time after time, Brazil seems to be able to pick superb players from out of nowhere and make them the envy of the world. Brazil's honors from soccer competitions are quite unmatched. It is the only nation that has played in all 14 World Cup tournaments, and in 1970 it became the first country to win the competition a third time.

THE PASSION Soccer enthusiasts around the world consider Brazil's most famous star, Pelé, to be the greatest player of all time. A member of all three of Brazil's world championship teams, he scored more than 1,200 goals in national and international competitions. In Brazil's last championship triumph during the 1970 World Cup in Mexico, Pelé combined with such legends as Tostao, Rivelino, Gerson and Jairzinho to form a team most experts agree to be the greatest in history.

When Brazil's national team plays, the nation comes to a halt. Work stops, traffic disappears from the streets, even the beaches become deserted. Every television network broadcasts the match, along with several radio networks. Radio announcers break into the familiar extended cry of "goooooooooaaaaaal" when Brazil scores. Fireworks erupt across the skies and people pour into the streets to celebrate victory.

A match between Santa Cruz and Flamengo in colossal Maracana Stadium. Forty years ago, the stadium hosted an unheard of 200,000 spectators in the deciding match of the 1950 World Cup. Overwhelming favorites Brazil were beaten 2-1 by Uruguay, plunging the whole nation into mourning.

On a smaller scale, this same enthusiasm accompanies matches played almost every day throughout Brazil. There are countless leagues for children, teenagers and adults. Besides the regular game played on a grass field with 11 players to a side, Brazilians play beach soccer on the sand with seven to a side, and indoor soccer on a hard surface with six to a side. One league even plays soccer in cars, with drivers punching a huge balloon-like ball along an oversized field.

THE FLA-FLU RIVALRY Rivalries are common in Brazilian soccer, but few rivalries in the world can match the intensity during the clash of Rio de Janeiro's super clubs, Flamengo and Fluminense. Brazilians refer to this game as the "Fla-Flu."

Fans for the teams will assemble throughout the city the morning of the game. Dressed in their teams' colors and carrying team flags, they dance and sing from the moment they gather. As the afternoon progresses, thousands of chanting supporters converge on Rio's mammoth Maracana Stadium, which will fill to its capacity of 155,000. The red and black shirts of Flamengo fans color one side of the stadium, while the red, white and green of Fluminense dominate the other.

By the time the teams take to the field in the late afternoon, the samba beat has already whipped the fans into a frenzy. They greet the players with an explosion of fireworks and a sea of waving flags. Flamengo fans throw confetti while Fluminense supporters heave talcum powder into the air. All eyes are focused on the field when the game begins. Like a wave, noise rises and falls from one end of the stadium to the other as the teams take turns dictating the play. The wave of noise crests when a goal is scored. Players on the field and fans in the stands leap into the air and exchange hugs. The flags and fireworks reappear.

At the end of the game, the losing team's supporters fold up their flags, put away their drumsticks and head home in sorrow. The winners take their party to the streets, hang their flags out of windows, honk car horns and keep the samba beat throughout the night. Radio stations will replay narratives of the goals. Monday newspapers will offer diagrams depicting how each was scored, along with commentaries on the performance of each player, coach and referee. Everywhere, the discussion of the game will not end … until the next Sunday's feature match.

One of the "must see" attractions of a visit to Brazil is a soccer match. Brazilian fans are known to be some of the most fanatical and enthusiastic in the world. Organized groups of supporters wave banners and can break out into song and dance with unbridled fervor at any time during the match. Even if the game is boring, the fan-watching is in itself a real treat.

SAND

Most of Brazil's population live within a short bus ride from the ocean. For these people, the beach is a part of daily life.

Brazilians take great pride in the fact that their beaches are open to all—in many places, the law prohibits private ownership of any part of the beach. Some sociologists even attribute the relative lack of tension between Brazil's classes to the "democracy" of the beach. When a man is on the beach in his bathing suit, they theorize, you don't know if he is upper class or lower class. They conclude that as long as the poor can freely mingle with the wealthy on the beach, they do not feel oppressed.

In practice, however, groups with different interests concentrate in their own stretch of the beach, informally dividing the sand into little communities. In Rio de Janeiro, artists and intellectuals frequent one area, members of a political party will regularly meet in another. Families with small children stay in one place, teenagers hang around another. The best surfers convene on one stretch, the best volleyball games are found in another. The regulars in the different patches get to know each other; making a trip to the beach is an opportunity to catch up with the latest news and gossip.

Early in the morning, people come to the beach for daily exercises. Lifeguards lead group calisthenic sessions, but the favorite form of exercising is the "Cooper Test," a 2.5-mile run named after an American doctor who was one of the early advocates of jogging. Signs along the beaches in many cities mark out the distances, and runners crowd the sidewalks in the early mornings and late afternoons.

Above: **Rio de Janeiro's famed Ipanema Beach. Ipanema ("Dangerous Waters") and its neighborhood are considered the center of Rio's style and culture, and boast one of the most expensive stretches of real estate in the world.**

Opposite: **A colorful Carnival in progress on a beach in Salvador.**

A VIEW FROM THE SAND

When the sun gets higher in the sky, sunbathers begin to arrive. During the week, many Brazilians will take a quick trip to the beach during their lunch breaks.

On a sunny weekend, thousands will cram the beaches. Most of them lie on the sand and relax, but it is hardly a quiet atmosphere. Vendors march up and down selling sweets, Brazilian fruit juices, hot coffee, a local brand of tea called *maté*, soft drinks, ice cream and hot dogs, not to mention an array of beach knick-knacks.

Games are played everywhere—soccer and volleyball grounds are marked off, complete with makeshift goalposts and nets; children fly bird-shaped kites; rubber balls are hit back and forth with paddles; bare hands are used to swat a *peteca* (a device consisting of long feathers weighted by a bundle of sand wrapped in leather).

Before going home, beach-goers will stop at one of the open-air cafés along the beach for a drink or a quick bite to eat.

Gradually, the afternoon crowd gives way to the night crowd. Couples stroll along the sand holding hands. The boardwalk in many cities becomes an outdoor arts fair, with artisans selling goods from paintings to woven hammocks. Music and conversation continue in the open-air cafés until late at night.

A beach vendor selling hats and suntan oil.

SPONTANEITY

During Carnival, samba is all the average Brazilian has on his or her mind. During the rest of the year, samba is never far from their thoughts. Anytime a group of Brazilians get together, be it on the beach, in a bus, at a restaurant, or inside a soccer stadium, if there's a can to tap or a box of matches to shake, a samba beat is likely to start.

A group of Brazilian researchers in the Antarctica said that they survived the unfamiliar freezing temperatures by warming up with a daily improvized samba session.

When they are not making their own music, Brazilians love to dance to music played by others. Even in small farming communities of the southern and northeastern interior, you can count on finding somewhere to dance on any given night.

Capoeira dancers performing on Ipanema Beach. It is a martial arts dance that was first introduced by slaves. Told to stop by their masters, the slaves disguised this foot-fighting technique, presenting it instead as a dance and thereby preserving a cultural art form.

MUSICAL FEVER

In a major city like Rio de Janeiro, the choice for samba is staggering. The large samba schools raise money and practice for the annual Carnival parade by holding samba parties at their headquarters all year round. Those performances draw huge crowds, but smaller bands play samba music in a cozier atmosphere in many nightclubs around town.

String bands playing *choro* music don't match the samba beat, but still provide lively dance music. Another option is the *gafieira*, a dance hall where Brazilian-style ballroom dancing is practiced. The *maxixe*, a favorite in the *gafieira*, combines the rapid rhythms of African and Latin music with the steps of a European polka. Watching the couples swerve around the floor can make viewers dizzy.

Some clubs feature *frevo* dancing, a style Brazilians in the northeast prefer over samba during Carnival. Lovers of music from the northeast can choose other night spots where *forro* bands perform. The accordion is the main instrument for this kind of music, the favorite of the *sertão* region. Urban Brazilians sometimes joke about *forro* music, much the same way some Americans do about hillbilly music.

As if homegrown music is not enough, Brazilians also love imported music. Dancers pack discos, rock and roll halls and jazz clubs.

One of the biggest crowds in the history of Rio de Janeiro's giant soccer stadium came to see a Frank Sinatra concert.

An afternoon rock and roll concert.

THE SOAPS

Television has joined music, soccer and the beach as a cornerstone of Brazilian leisure. TV Globo, Brazil's largest network, is the fourth largest in the world. Only the three principal American networks operate more stations. Four smaller networks also operate in Brazil.

Most of the shows on the air are made in Brazil. The most popular are the *telenovelas*, long-running serials aired during prime time. These programs can be seen every night, but TV Globo's feature show, the one bringing together the most stars and the best production team, comes on the air every weeknight at 8:30. Just as life stops for soccer games on Sundays, more and more Brazilians refuse to schedule anything during the week at this time.

One survey suggested that 70 million people—8 out of every 10 Brazilian television viewers—closely followed a recent TV Globo prime time *novela*. That show, like others preceding it, introduced new slang and phrases into the Brazilian language, and new fashions into Brazilian dress codes.

Although they portray Brazilian characters in Brazilian settings, TV Globo's serials have become hits all over the world. They have been dubbed, for example, into Italian for Roman audiences and into Chinese for Singapore viewers.

The man in the red cap seems as immersed in the drama on television as the children next to him.

103

FESTIVALS

"E CARNAVAL!" IT'S CARNIVAL TIME! Every year this cry fills the air to start a four-day national holiday. Everyone forgets his or her problems, pulls on a costume, and dances to the rhythms of samba, *frevo* and *lambada* music.

Brazilians adore music, dancing and partying. Festive parties are a part of many religious festivals, but the biggest party of all is the Carnival. Dating back to early Christian times, this event began as a last chance to frolic and feast before the beginning of Lent. While carnivals are celebrated in various countries around the world, no nation matches the frenzy and the excitement of Carnival in Brazil.

Carnival takes place during late February or early March. Traditionally, it starts the Sunday before the beginning of Lent and ends on Ash Wednesday, but Brazilians extend the party to last at least a week. During this period, mayors ceremonially hand over the keys of their cities to King Momo, an ancient Greek god of mockery and jest.

Opposite and below: **Carnival is deeply rooted in ethnic and racial heritage. Some say the word "carnival" comes from the Italian *Carne Vale*, which means "farewell to meat," since it marks the last days before Lenten abstinence; others say it is derived from the Latin *Carrum Novalis*, meaning Roman festival float.**

Pretty in pink: a section of the Manqueira Samba School performing their routines.

CARNIVAL IN RIO DE JANEIRO

The most famous festivities take place in Rio de Janeiro. The biggest event is the parade of the 26 best *escolas de samba*, or samba schools, along the Sambadrome, a street lined with grandstands. For three nights, thousands watch the elaborately costumed participants dance and sing their way down the parade route.

On Ash Wednesday, an official jury announces its pick as the best school in that year's parade and the winner's celebration extends the Carnival joy through the weekend.

Dancing is not restricted to the Sambadrome. Costumed merrymakers called *foliões* take over the city streets, their dress code varying from clown outfits to swimwear. Groups wearing the same costumes make up

a *bloco*. The most well known is the *Bloco das Piranhas*, a group of men who take to the streets every year dressed as women. The *blocos* and the individual *foliões* fall in behind various small samba bands which roam on foot or in a car, and spontaneous street parties may erupt anywhere.

Private clubs throw extravagant parties attended by as many as 10,000 people. The most famous is the "Night In Baghdad" theme ball on the last night of the Carnival. Party-goers wear either a tuxedo or a costume. In the heat of the crammed ballroom, most opt for the latter.

Samba music and dancing keep the temperature high from midnight until well past breakfast the next morning.

Samba dancers decorate the occasion with baskets of flowers and fruit while parading along the Sambadrome. Dancers train the whole year for Carnival, which lasts only a few days.

CARNIVAL IN SALVADOR AND RECIFE

Less vibrant *escola de samba* parades take place in other cities, but the favorite Carnival spots after Rio are in the northeast. The street celebrations in Salvador da Bahia and Recife are almost as intense.

Frevo music replaces the samba as the favorite. Based on African rhythms, it originated in Recife. Today, the city's expert *frevo* dancers perform in traditional fashion, wearing knee-length pants, long stockings, baggy shirts and waving bright umbrellas.

Children dressed as clowns take to the streets for a party .

The trademark of Salvador's Carnival is a specially equiped truck called the *Trio Eletrico*. Loudspeakers lining the sides of this truck blast music played by a band on its top. The crowds following the truck dance to various types of music, from the traditional *frevo* to the more recent *deboche* or *lambada*. These newer rhythms draw upon samba, *frevo* and outside influences such as Reggae and rock and roll music.

Afoxés also march through the streets of Salvador during Carnival. Made up of followers of African religions, they sprinkle lavender cologne on the crowd and sing sacred songs, often in African languages. Curiously, one *afoxé* is named the Sons of Gandhi, after the famous leader of India.

Recife has neither samba schools nor *trio eletricos*, but there is no shortage of *frevo* bands and costumed *blocos* along its streets. It also has its *maracatu* marches. First practiced by slaves longing for their homeland, black groups still carry out this re-enactment of the royal procession of an African king. Other groups wear feathered headdresses and paint their faces to perform the *caboclinho*, a frenetic dance learned from Indians.

An African dance performed in Salvador.

ESCOLAS DE SAMBA

It's Carnival, and one of Rio's best *escolas de samba* has filled the mile-long Sambadrome. The school's 3,000 dancers sing and swing to a samba beat pounded out by a 250-man percussion section. Gigantic floats break them up into distinct sections, each defined by bright costumes. For an hour and a half, this wave of color and sound makes its way along the avenue. The samba schools take turns parading before huge crowds. Starting at around 8 p.m., they go on until at least 9 the next morning.

The schools are actually neighborhood associations, most coming from the poorer areas of the city. All year long, members volunteer their time to put together the extravagant costumes and floats, and to practice dancing and singing. Each school's presentation is built around a theme song, called a *samba enredo*. Through the floats and the costumes, they build this theme into a story.

Generally, the theme is Brazilian folklore or history. Occasionally, it makes a humorous comment on modern life. One group's 1990 theme revolved around a Rio de Janeiro neighborhood known for its sale of stolen property. The percussion section wore police uniforms while some of the costumes and floats portrayed jails, weapons, car tires and television sets.

The structure of each parade follows a set formula. First comes the *Abre Alas* or opening wing. Accompanied by the initial float, this group introduces the main theme. A line of gentlemen in dark suits follows. They are the school's figurative board of directors, intended to add an air of dignity to the fun.

The samba starts in earnest with the arrival of the *Mestre Sala* and *Porta Bandeira*, the school's dance master and flag bearer. The different wings follow, separated by floats and groups of *passistas*, the school's most skilled samba dancers, performing elaborate dance steps and acrobatic leaps.

Each school also features a *baiana* wing, where black women in traditional clothing celebrate the African origin of the Brazilian samba. The percussion section, called the *bateria*, starts near the front but pulls up along the avenue for the last group of dancers to catch up so that they can keep up with the beat.

NATIONAL HOLIDAYS

Jan 1   — New Year's Day
Feb/Mar   — Carnival (4 days)
Mar/Apr   — Good Friday and Easter Sunday
Apr 21   — Tiradentes Day (honors a famous Brazilian patriot)
May 1   — Labor Day
May/Jun   — Corpus Christi
Sep 7   — Independence Day
Oct 12   — Our Lady of Aparecida (patron saint of Brazil)
Nov 2   — All Souls Day
Nov 15   — Proclamation of the Republic
Dec 25   — Christmas

OKTOBERFEST

The biggest festival in the south of Brazil has nothing to do with Africa or the Catholic Church. The Oktoberfest in Blumenau, Santa Catarina, started only in 1982, is now the world's second largest beer festival. In 1988, over a million people drank 200,000 gallons of beer during the 16-day event. Only the original Oktoberfest in Munich, Germany, outdoes that. German immigrants founded Blumenau, and during October, there is little evidence of the New World in the city. People listening to the polka bands, eating *wurst* with sauerkraut, or watching the blonde, blue-eyed girls serving beer in the *biergarten* would be sure they were in Germany.

RELIGIOUS FESTIVALS

Catholic holy days make up about half of Brazil's national holidays. The feast day of Brazil's patron saint, Nossa Senhora de Aparecida, is the most unique. In 1717, fishermen in the state of São Paulo found a statue of the Virgin Mary in a river. They built a chapel and a cult grew around the statue. Today, that chapel has become a huge basilica, sitting along the Rio-São Paulo highway. About eight million devotees visit the church each year, over a million during the month of October.

Nativity sets and Santa Claus are both a part of Christmas in Brazil. Instead of arriving through the chimney, children believe that *Papai Noel* comes in through the window and leaves presents in shoes left on the floor. More important than the gift-giving is the traditional Christmas Eve dinner, which brings together the entire extended family.

Numerous other religious days are observed across the country. The feast days of Saints Anthony (June 12), John (June 23) and Peter (June 28) fall together closely enough to justify two weeks of parties, called *festas juninas*. Party-goers dress in country style to attend outdoor parties, featuring Brazilian country music and cooking. Fireworks, bonfires and religious processions are other elements of the festivities. St. Anthony is the patron saint of single men and women, so staged wedding ceremonies are often played out on his feast day.

Many religious festivals are unique to different regions. New Year's Eve in Rio de Janeiro is the feast day of Iemanja, the African Mother of the Waters. At midnight, her followers flock to the beach to launch gifts on

A merry musician puts on a bright smile, depicting the overall attitude of Brazilians during the celebration of the nation's long list of festivals.

tiny boats. Tradition says that the goddess will not accept the gifts of those without virtue, so their boats will wash back to shore. To prevent this from happening, believers wade as far out as possible before releasing their offerings.

The same ceremony takes place in Salvador on February 2. On New Year's Day, Salvador joins other northeastern towns in celebrating the feast of Lord Jesus of the Navigators. A parade of colorfully decorated ships escorts a statue of Jesus Christ across the harbor, as sailors believe that their homage to the Lord will protect them from harm.

FOOD

BRAZIL'S FOOD MIRRORS ITS CULTURE. In preparing their meals, Brazilians use practices and ingredients introduced by European immigrants, African slaves and native Indians. As with culture, the degree of influence of each varies according to the region.

The two staples of the Brazilian diet are manioc flour and beans. Manioc comes from the cassava plant. Indians on the northeast coast cultivated this plant when the Portuguese first arrived in Brazil.

The Portuguese brought beans with them, as well as rice, sugarcane and coffee. Traders on their way back from the Far East delivered cloves, cinammon and other spices. African slaves introduced bananas and a type of palm oil called *dendê*. *Dendê* oil remains a key ingredient in the typical dishes of the northeast.

Opposite: **A vegetable market on a street in historical Ouro Preto.**

Left: **A fisherman's family comes together to have a meal.**

FEIJOADA

Despite the regional differences, there is one dish that brings the country together. In many restaurants and homes, the Saturday *feijoada* is a weekly ritual.

The classic *feijoada* served in Rio de Janeiro combines black beans and various types of dried and smoked meats. This meal has developed with help from all three of Brazil's ethnic roots. Along with rice, a fried manioc flour dish called *farofa* is the main complement of the *feijoada*. The African contribution comes from history.

Slaves gave Brazil the original *feijoada* recipe. In colonial days, the master kept the best cuts of the meat for his family, giving his slaves leftovers like pig's feet or beef tongue. The slaves threw these into a pot with their beans, added onions, garlic and a few other spices and created a concoction that eventually caught the master's attention.

Today, many restaurants serve two types of *feijoada*: *feijoada tipica* contains the traditional meats, including eyes, ears, tongues and tails; *feijoada moderna* sticks to more conventional cuts such as pork loins and beef brisket. Made either way, the end result is a delicious meal over which Brazilians will linger for two to three hours.

They warm up with a *caiprinha*, an alcoholic drink with lime, sugar, and *cachaça*—a liquor distilled from sugarcane. The main meal follows: a helping or two of the beans, meat, rice, *farofa*, fresh oranges and fried chopped kale will leave those eating in the mood to relax for the rest of the day.

The simple *feijoada,* in all its elegance. The humble bean recipe has been crowned Brazil's national dish.

116

BAHIAN FOOD

Bahia is home to Brazil's most distinctive cuisine: here, Portuguese and African practices combined with seafood and the tropical food of the northeast coast to produce a unique way of cooking.

To foreigners, Bahian food does not always look appetizing. Its ingredients are usually mashed and mixed in one pot, and served over rice, manioc or corn meal. But the rich taste from ingredients— including *dendê* oil, coconut milk, dried shrimp or fish, crabmeat and cashew nuts—soon wins over

A *baiana* selling—and sampling—her wares in an open-air market. *Baianas* (Bahian women) are considered Brazil's best bakers of sweet food.

those who try it. The piquant taste of *malagueta* chili peppers balances the richness of these flavors. For those who like their food extra spicy, a bowl of pepper usually accompanies a Bahian dish.

Baianas dressed in white sell these dishes along the streets of cities like Salvador. Local favorites include:

—*moqueca*: a stew built around *dendê* oil, coconut milk, fish or shrimp and spiced by *malagueta* peppers, garlic and cloves.

—*vatapá*: also a stew with ingredients similar to those in *moqueca*, but thicker because manioc flour is added. The addition of ginger in the place of cloves also changes the taste.

—*caruru*: this dish combines shrimp with the vegetable okra. The two are boiled in water, spiced by onions and peppers, then mixed with *dendê* oil.

—*acarajé*: this favorite fast food is the rough equivalent of an American burger. A *baiana* soaks and removes the skin from local *fradinho* beans, mashes them together, adds diced shrimp and onions, then fries the mixture in *dendê* oil.

PREPARING MANIOC FLOUR

Farmers in the north and northeast still prepare manioc flour from the roots of the cassava plant, using the same procedure native Indians have been using for 400 years. As the illustration shows, the technology they employ has advanced, but not much.

After the roots have been picked and peeled, they are chopped in a grinder called a *cevadeira* (1). Metal blades inside this grinder are moved by turning a wheel.

Yanomami Indians grating manioc flour to make soup for 100 guests.

The roots contain poisonous prussic acid. To extract this poison, a levered press (2) pounds the chopped cassava. The liquid which runs off holds the acid, and a paste is left behind. This paste is run through a sieve to separate the thicker part, called *crueira*. This is used to feed cattle.

The thin paste is boiled in an open pot (3) and stirred constantly until it has been roasted dry. This powder is manioc flour.

Indians shooting for fish with bow and arrow at the Xingu National Park.

OTHER REGIONAL FOODS

Seafood is the favorite food in most of the northern region. *Sururu*, a clam stew prepared in oyster sauce, and stuffed crab are favorite dishes in the state of Pernambuco. *Pirão*, a porridge prepared with manioc and fish broth, often accompanies seafood.

Fresh meat and fish can be hard to come by in the hot northeastern *sertão*, so *carne de sol* (dried salted meat) is a staple. This type of meat does not need to be refrigerated. After slaughtering a cow, ranchers rub salt into the meat and hang it on racks to dry in the sun and wind. Another favorite in the *sertão* is the *buchada*, a dish made from goat's liver, heart and tripe. If prepared traditionally, the ingredients are stuffed into a goat's stomach, sewed shut and cooked for four to five hours.

The influence of native Indians is still strong in the north, as the names of many dishes reveal. Residents of the states of Pará and Amazonas often eat fresh *pirarucu* and *tucunare* fish served with a manioc sauce called *tucupi*. They also enjoy a number of fruits unique to the Amazon.

In the south, *churrasco* is the most popular meal: meat on a spit slowly grilled and basted with salt water for flavor. Brazilians either cook *churrascos* at home, or they go to *churrascaria* restaurants, where the price of a meal pays for all you can eat.

THE FRUITS OF BRAZIL

Sapotis, guavas, *fruta-de-conde*, *maracujá*, *pitanga*, *umbu*, *jaca*, *guaraná* … the forests of Brazil are a treasure chest of exquisite fruits.

Ice cream shops in cities like Belem in Pará advertise 99 flavors. But an American or European visitor would have a hard time identifying most of them. Here are just a few examples of the fruits that would be featured:

Açaí: the fruit of a palm tree called the *açaizeiro*, this is common in Amazonas and Pará. It is usually mixed with sugar and served in a gourd, or else used to make wine. Northerners insist that any visitor who drinks *açai* wine will visit the region again.

Graviola: from the same family as the pineapple, this oval-shaped fruit weighs one to two pounds. A white, creamy meat and fine dark seeds lie inside its pale green skin. It tastes like a cross between a banana and a pineapple.

Jabuticaba: a red or black berry that originally grew in the wild, this is now cultivated in different parts of Brazil. Its sweet, white pulp is used to make pies, jellies or wine.

Jaca: this is the jackfruit from Southeast Asia. Traders brought it to Brazil in the 18th century, and it thrives in the tropical climate. The fruit can weigh up to 40 pounds, but its pulp tastes rather sour. Brazilians use the pulp to make sweets or jellies, and roast the seeds to eat.

Goiaba: called "guava" in English, this yellow, pear-shaped fruit is grown everywhere in the country. One of their favorite fruits, Brazilians believe it stimulates the appetite if eaten before a meal, and helps digestion if eaten afterward.

Jenipapo: about the size of an apple, this light brown fruit originated in the Antilles. It thrives in Brazil's north, where Indians use its dark pulp to blacken their faces. When ripe, the *jenipapo* skin is thin and soft, and the watery pulp has a sweet and sour taste.

CUSTOMS

Breakfast is usually a light meal for most Brazilians, with some fruit accompanying buttered bread and coffee. Lunch, generally the biggest meal of the day, regularly takes up to two hours. Many employers grant extended lunch breaks to allow workers to enjoy this meal at home. Dinner is served quite late, usually around 8.30 at night. In between lunch and dinner, many people have a *lanche*, a small snack along with a coffee or juice.

Like good grammar, Brazilians consider good table manners to be a sign of a good education, and hence of good social standing. Those with good manners do not use bare hands to pick up food. They use a fork and knife for everything, including apples, oranges, sandwiches, chicken legs and pizzas. A growing number of American-style fast food restaurants is gradually changing this rule, but many carefully wrap a napkin around their hamburgers.

Children may eat an ice cream cone while walking down the street, but Brazilians consider it rude for an adult to eat in public. Those who buy food from a streetside vendor usually eat it on the spot. This habit stems from the belief that food should be shared. Anytime a Brazilian is eating, whether it be a meal at home or a candy bar on the beach, he will offer to share with any friend that comes along. When offered food, it is considered rude to say no without offering a good excuse. Similarly, hosts are expected to provide more than enough food for their guests, and guests are expected to try their best to eat all of it.

Accompanied by junior's brawling at the far end of the table, a Brazilian family gathers to eat.

DRINKS

Coffee is Brazil's national drink. A *cafézinho* is a mandatory part of any social event, whether it be lunch with the family at home, or a business meeting in the office. *Cafézinho* means "little coffee," and this very strong brew is served in a cup one-third the size of an American coffee cup. Brazilians add lots of sugar to counter the strength of the coffee.

Business people always start their meetings by drinking a *cafézinho*, during which they have a friendly chat. Serious talks only begin

A popular *cafézinho* bar and its patrons.

when the cups are empty. The opposite occurs during meals, when the *cafézinho* comes after the meal is finished. While food is on the table, conversation is superficial, but over the little cup, the earnest discussions can begin.

Good drink and conversation are trademarks of the sidewalk bars and cafés found on almost every street corner. Whether stopping by on the way home from the beach, or meeting up with friends after dinner, Brazilians spend a lot of time here. They drink fruit juices such as coconut milk or freshly-squeezed mango, and fruit milkshakes. Popular milkshakes use ingredients such as raw oatmeal, avocado, papaya and banana. *Guarana*, a unique Brazilian soft drink, is made from a small tropical fruit. Beer and *cachaça* are popular at night. Bartenders combine *cachaça* with different fruits to make drinks called *batidas*.

Wine is becoming increasingly popular. Almost all of Brazil's wine comes from Rio Grande do Sul, where vineyards started by Italian immigrants continue to improve the quality of their product.

BRAZIL

N

VENEZUELA

GUYANA

SURINAM

FR. GUIANA

COLOMBIA

ATLANTIC OCEAN

Equator

Japurá

Negro

Amazonas

● Manaus

● Belém

● São Luís

Parnaíba

● Fortaleza

Amazonas

Madeira

Aripuanã

Tapajós

Xingu

Natal ●

João Pessoa ●
Recife

Paulistana ●

Araguaia

Tocantins

São Francisco

Maceió ●

Guaporé

Salvador ●

PERU

BOLIVIA

● **Brasília**

Paraguay

● Belo Horizonte

PARAGUAY

Paraná

● Ribeirão Prêto

Rio de Janeiro ●
● Niterói

São Paulo ●

● Santos

PACIFIC OCEAN

CHILE

Curitiba ●

Tropic of Capricorn

Uruguay

SOUTH ATLANTIC OCEAN

ARGENTINA

● Pôrto Alegre

URUGUAY

● Rio Grande do Sul

124

International Boundary
Tropic of Capricorn
Equator
Capital
City
River

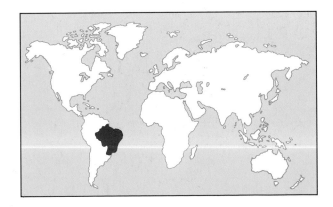

QUICK NOTES

LAND AREA
3.3 million square miles

POPULATION
150 million

CAPITAL
Brasília

STATES
Acre, Alagoas, Amapa, Amazonas, Bahia, Ceara, Distrito Federal, Espirito Santo, Goiás, Maranhão, Mato Grosso, Mato Grosso do Sul, Minas Gerais, Pará, Paraiba, Paraná, Pernambuco, Piaui, Rio de Janeiro, Rio Grande do Norte, Rio Grande do Sul, Rondônia, Roraima, Santa Catarina, São Paulo, Sergipe, Tocantins.

MAJOR RIVER
The Amazon

HIGHEST POINT
Mt. Bandeira (9,480 feet)

CLIMATE
Temperatures and rainfall vary for different parts of the country. In the north, it is humid with heavy rainfall all year round. In the coastal areas, it is hot, with slightly less rainfall. In the central regions, it is semi-humid and is hot and wet in the summer (the seasons are inverted in the Southern Hemisphere—summer in the USA is winter in Brazil) and drier and cooler in the winter. In the south, it is humid with regular rainfall and even occasional snowfall and frosts.

NATIONAL LANGUAGE
Portuguese

MAJOR RELIGION
Christianity

CURRENCY
Cruzeiro

MAIN EXPORTS
Coffee, orange juice, soybeans, cocoa, military weapons, cars, aircrafts.

IMPORTANT ANNIVERSARIES
February/March, Carnival; April 21, Tiradentes Day—honors a famous Brazilian patriot; May/June, Corpus Christi; September 7, Independence Day; October 12, Nossa Senhora de Aparecida—honoring Brazil's patron saint; November 15, Proclamation of the Republic.

MAJOR POLITICAL LEADERS
Dom Pedro II—emperor of Brazil. His leadership gave the country its longest continuous period of political stability. Brazil's most popular leader ever was overthrown and exiled in 1889 because his policies favored the common man and not the elite or the army.

Getúlio Vargas—president who was popular with the urban population and not with the rural barons and landowners.

Juscelino Kubitschek—dynamic president who built Brasília from scratch but, as a result, left the country in serious trouble with debt and inflation.

GLOSSARY

baiana	Woman from the northern state of Bahia.
bandeirante	Early explorers of Brazil's interior regions from the state of São Paulo.
caboclo	Brazilian of mixed blood, with European and Indian ancestry.
cafuso	Brazilian of mixed blood, with African and Indian ancestry.
candomblé	African religion adherents of which believe in the possession of human participants by supernatural spirits.
carioca	A resident of Rio de Janeiro.
cassava	The plant from which manioc flour is extracted.
dendê	A type of palm tree; oil from it is a key ingredient in Bahian cooking.
favela	Slums in Brazilian cities.
gaucho	Cowboy of Brazil's southern plains; commonly used to refer to a resident of the state of Rio Grande do Sul.
jeito	A way—the slang for describing a knack for completing difficult tasks.
mulatto	Brazilian of mixed blood, with European and African ancestry.
samba	A style of music and dance brought to Brazil from Africa.
sertão	Dry and arid land in Brazil's northeast.

BIBLIOGRAPHY

Harrison, Phyllis: *Behaving Brazilian: A Comparison of Brazilian and North American Social Behavior*, Newbury House Publishers, New York, 1983.

Sterling, Tom: *The Amazon*, Time-Life Books, Amsterdam, 1973.

Taylor, Edwin (editor): *Insight Guides: Brazil*, APA Publications, Singapore, 1989.

Wagley, Charles: *An Introduction to Brazil*, Columbia University Press, New York, 1971.

INDEX

Picture Credits